PRODUCTIVITY INDICES

Dedicated to Bernice

Productivity Indices

Methods and Applications

M. S. SILVER

Lecturer in Industrial Economics and Statistics,
School of Management
University of Bath

Gower

Published by
Gower Publishing Company Limited,
Gower House, Croft Road, Aldershot, Hampshire GU11 3HR, England

and

Gower Publishing Company,
Old Post Road, Brookfield, Vermont 05036, U.S.A.

British Library Cataloguing in Publication Data
———

Silver, M.S.
  Productivity indices
  1. Industrial productivity——Measurement
  I. Title
  338'.06'0287   HD56.25

ISBN 0-566-00724-X

Printed in Great Britain by
Biddles Ltd, Guildford, Surrey

Contents

Preface

This book outlines a framework for aggregate productivity measurement and analysis at the plant/organisational level. My interest in productivity analysis originated in studies I undertook involving the analysis of production and productivity changes in the Tanzanian and Iranian economies. Whilst the principles governing the measurement and interpretation of productivity changes for macroeconomic analysis are not coterminous with those pertaining to decision-making requirements at the organisational level, many similar considerations remain. This study develops a set of indicators under an analytical framework which is designed to aid in the interpretation of aggregate (organisational) productivity measures. In a manner akin to financial accounts it provides for the organisation a set of quantitative indicators of a more complex reality. The indicators developed are devised to aid in discerning features of, and trends in, production relationships. Such information is argued to be pertinent to decision-making.

My thinking on productivity over the years has been influenced by, and benefited from, discussions with Zbigniew Kmietowicz (University of Leeds), Paul Golder (University of Aston) and Dudley Jackson (now at the University of Wollongong). In particular, the vast majority of the second chapter stemmed from a working paper co-authored by Dudley Jackson. I wish to thank John Wiley and Sons Ltd for permission to reproduce my article published in **Managerial and Decision Economics**, 3, 4, 1982 in Chapter 3, and the West Midlands Regional Management Centre for permission to reproduce my article published in their **Review**, 2, 3, 1982/83 as Appendix II. This book is also intended to serve as an exploratory framework for an Economic and Social Research Council (ESRC) funded research project on potential productivity (with Alan Bennett) and the support of the ESRC is, therefore, acknowledged. I was fortunate enough to receive superb secretarial support from Diane Milton, whom I thank. Finally, I thank my wife, Bernice, for her encouragement and patience. Any errors remain, of course, my responsibility.

Mick Silver
University of Bath

January 1984

Introduction

It is not uncommon for economic and business pundits to emphasise the need to increase productivity to overcome the problems of British industry. Ignoring the somewhat tautological element in such pleas, the advocate for improving productivity usually finds many supporters. Behind the term 'improved productivity' is a hint of increased output from a more efficient utilisation of inputs to the production process. Depending, to some extent, on the political beliefs of the advocate a more efficient utilisation of inputs may be considered to stem from one or more of: increased effort from existing labour and more flexibility by labour within the working environment, improved organisation of the production process, improved administration by management, increased capital services per employee through the purchase of more up-to-date machines and equipment. In this latter case a change in the ratio of capital to labour services may be considered which requires the purchase of additional capital or replacement of existing capital for 'new' capital embodying some technological improvements. This differs from economies of scale, or an improved organisation of the production process for which no extra direct financial cost is being incurred by the organisation. More than proportionate output increases stem from input increases like 'manna from heaven'. However, if the manna has a price tag attached, say by a work study group, the additional (discounted) value of output arising from the reorganisation of the work process should be more than the price charged for the work study to be undertaken (including disruption costs etc). Improved productivity may be deemed to be 'efficient' in this sense when the above condition is met. Similarly, the price of the replacement capital must exceed its expected, additional (discounted) contribution to the value of output.

Improved labour productivity may stem from increased 'effort' by employees, though if attained through a financial incentive scheme similar considerations to those noted above are required. Even if increased effort results from overt supervision, pressure and regular monitoring, then the costs to the organisation of maintaining such a system, in addition to the costs (hiring, retraining) of wastage and absenteeism, should be taken into account and the social costs to the individual at least noted.

Increased output may thus stem from a number of sources. The effects of increased effort, reorganisation of the work process, economies of scale, technological change have been noted. Other sources include improved 'quality' of employees through experience, training and education, better utilisation of capital and labour, less 'wear and tear' on capital, changes in the capital to labour ratio. A further source would be to increase the services supplied by labour through increasing hours worked (overtime). Again the additional output and cost from overtime may be compared with the relative output and costs (including hiring, training and fixed capital requirements and impact on flexibility and control) of the alternative of taking on more employees.

Additions to outputs from different input sources (marginal products) may be derived from the coefficients of a properly specified production function and then compared with the relative prices of additional units of inputs. The estimation of production functions requires some statistical expertise and a range of often unrealistic assumptions. Furthermore, such estimates of stable coefficients may be ill suited for monitoring short-term changes in the relationships between outputs and inputs. In view of this an index number approach is proposed based on the economic theory of index numbers which, whilst borrowing many concepts from the elegant neo-classical economic theory immersed in production function work, provides an operational procedure for managerial decision-making. Dismissing economic theory does not, of course, make the assumptions go away. However, it is argued that in any decision to change production by the aforementioned sources, the comparison between expected contribution and costs are (should be) an implicit element. By establishing a framework which isolates the need for such an analytical process, a systematic element is introduced into decision-making. Emphasis is given to the use of judgement at the organisational/plant level and the ability to discern the effects of changes in inputs under controlled conditions at the shop level. When forming part of a meaningful framework such information (not amenable to econometric analysis) becomes invaluable. Adjustments at the macro level are often crude, since the economist has to apply some form of 'average' or expected pattern to, for example, capacity utilisation derived from comparing the difference between an estimated optimum level based on, say, fitting a trend to peak levels in output data. At the plant level the level of capacity utilisation of capital may well be discerned from, for example, some performance characteristic of the machine relative to the manufacturer of the capital goods' specification, experience with the machine, and an 'intimate' knowledge of factors which may have 'upset' the production process.

However, let us return to productivity. So far, some importance has been attached to a delineation by source of contributions to production changes. Yet what of our faithful measures, labour productivity, capital productivity? Such partial measures can only tell part of the story. Labour productivity as measured by output per employee is not only influenced by changes in the level of capital utilisation, 'wear and tear' on capital and the ratio of capital stock to labour stock, but also by factors which affect the flow of labour services from a given stock of labour, (i.e. effort, experience, etc.). As such labour productivity may fall if the capital to labour ratio falls. Yet if such a process arises because the additional product from capital relative to labour is less than the additional price of capital relative to labour, then the fall in labour productivity is not 'bad' in the sense noted above. The approach proposed in this book is to set up an accounting framework which seeks to account for the sources of production changes. Accounting for change includes reference not only to physical output being 'explained' in terms of contributions by physical inputs, but also the discerning of price, value and terms-of-trade changes for inputs and outputs which influence the benefits derived from changes in production. Once the sources of production changes have been isolated in a descriptive sense, a prescriptive inference exists in that the framework leads to a consideration of the possibility of discerning, potential sources for increasing the contribution of inputs to outputs. Conventional measures of ratios of money variables (e.g. output to labour costs) or physical variables (e.g. quantity produced to number of employees) are thus special cases of this more general framework; inadequate when considered alone.

Economic theory allows us to ascertain conditions for the efficient allocation of resources. The econometric estimation of production functions (or the dual cost functions) and use of the calculus is impractical operationally. Questions of expertise and computing facilities apart the stability of coefficients cannot be guaranteed over the time periods required given the number of sources (variables) under analysis (skills of labour, types of capital, etc.). Such an analysis considers decision-making parameters derived from estimated relationships over a period of time, when the concern of management might be with recent changes which demand quite different considerations. The framework outlined will be based on the economic theory of index numbers which will be argued to provide a more operational system of productivity analysis. Index number formulae corresponding to flexible functional forms will be utilised to minimise errors arising from assumptions as to the form of the 'black box' of the production function. Chaining of such formulae will be advocated to ensure the parameters of the production function implied by a particular index number are not out-of-date, but can change in response to changes in the production configuration of the organisation. Guidelines will be outlined whereby management may adjust the weighting system to account for market imperfections. Unlike aggregate econometric analysis the system will be enhanced by the identification of productivity benefits accruing from new developments when such effects can be isolated in a controlled environment at the shop level.

The proposed framework will, however, be seen to suffer from a number of problems. Accounting for changes in output by recourse to changes in specific inputs requires some form of weighting system to enable input changes (including technology change) to add up to output changes. Conditions may be derived from economic theory based on the effects on output of infinitesimal changes in specific inputs, such changes taking place independently of other inputs. Assumptions that organisations can efficiently control, and are aware of changes which may lead to deviations from cost-minimisation policies may be invoked. (Unless we are to believe that the 'invisible hand' of competition will ensure all firms make decisions which satisfy cost minimisation goals.) A number of elements which are difficult to quantify may be excluded or guesstimates derived (for example labour relations, style of decision-making, attitudes and work practices). It must be stressed that it is not intended, nor is it possible, to isolate all sources of inputs to explain changes in outputs. Too many non-quantifiable elements impose including 'morale', institutional constraints and so forth. However, our concern is that changes in policies which are aimed at these less quantifiable elements can at least be ascertained in terms of improved outputs relative to a level of quantifiable inputs. It is further argued that a framework for the systematic analysis of quantifiable elements rather than 'ad hoc' principles should be welcomed given their not unimportant contribution to the production process. A knowledge of the relationship between, and the monitoring of, changes in the volume of inputs and outputs is argued to be an important aspect of management since such information is necessary to identify whether changes need to be made to the administration of the production process. The monitoring of price and terms-of-trade changes is also essential in that such price changes provide the link between changes in the benefits that accrue to the parties involved in the production process. Estimates of changes in the physical contribution of inputs and prices of inputs provide an empirical basis for the adjustment of production techniques to meet new (relative price) circumstances. Partial measures of, say output per employee (labour productivity) obscure rather than help, since they incorporate the effects of so many other factors. In using such partial measures aggregation problems may be minimised, yet they beg so many questions in their interpretation in terms of the effects and relative importance of other factors, that a need to account for change by recourse to (weighted) inputs of other factors is implicitly required. The manager told that labour productivity is falling, wants to know why. If the question "why?" incorporates a need to examine all factors influencing labour productivity and the relative importance of each factor it is better that a system of accounts with estimates of the effects of such factors is initially provided. Such accounts can note the basis of the estimates and areas of ignorance, providing a framework for analysis within which all factors pertinent to the analysis can be expressed 'warts (explicitly identified) and all'.

It should finally be noted that the system outlined is intended to represent changes in aggregate productivity, for an organisation or plant as a whole. In the same way that financial accounts are prepared to give an overview, the proposed productivity framework isolates pertinent features of an organisation's operation or performance. It is limited in its scope of concern (with generally quantifiable aspects of production and relative price relationships) and its focus on aggregate relationships. The source for such estimates may be derived from the shop floor and may induce improvements at this level. However, the framework, as with financial accounts, is intended to provide a tool for monitoring aggregate performance characteristics of an organisation which are considered to be essential to resource allocation within the organisation.

Chapter 1 explores the concept of productivity, shows how meaning and measurement are inter-related and provides an 'accounting for change' framework. The importance of measurement leads to a consideration in Chapters 2, 4 and 5 of the measurement of production, labour input and capital input respectively. Chapter 3 is concerned with the index number problems and outlines a framework based on the economic theory of index numbers. Appendix I outlines the features of the measurement of production at the UK, national level. Appendix II is concerned with management value added systems in general.

1 Productivity: meaning and measurement

The Production Function as a General Framework

Productivity is the relationship between a flow of output produced and the things which are used to achieve that flow of output. Correspondingly, changes in productivity refer to the relationship between changes in a flow of output and changes in the things used.

The production process may be represented as flows of capital services, labour services, the services from land, energy and raw materials conjoining to generate a flow of output. In mathematical shorthand:

$$Q = f(K, L, La, X_1, X_2 \ldots X_n) \qquad \ldots(1)$$

where Q is the flow of goods/services produced; K, L and La the flow of services provided by capital, labour and land respectively and X_1, X_2 ... X_n the bought-in inputs of energy and materials/services to the production process. Thus the flow of goods/services from a production process is a mathematical function of (or is determined by) the flow of inputs of capital, labour, land, energy and materials/services inputs to the production process. Such a relationship is referred to as a 'production function'.

By relating the flow of goods/services produced to any one, or a subset, of the variables on the right-hand side of the function given above **partial** (average) measures of productivity are provided. For example, let X_1 denote the input of fuel to the production process; thus Q/X_1 is the productivity of fuel. The productivity of fuel will vary between establishments or sectors of the economy as some establishments generate a greater flow of output from a unit input of fuel. The productivity of fuel for a particular establishment or sector may vary over time as the 'efficiency' with which fuel is utilised varies and/or as the type of activities vary; say, as a greater (or lesser) concentration of production is centred around processes (products) which are more conservative users of fuel for generating a given 'value' of output. The productivity of a particular input is of particular significance if that input is limited, since it is obviously important that as much production as possible is generated from that input. As we shall identify later, the relative prices of inputs to the production process provides (in theory for a cost minimisation goal) a mechanism by which scarce resources may be directed to particular uses.

In a similar manner the partial productivities of land, capital, labour and other inputs may be identified. One may argue that managerial skill, alternative methods of organising the work process including different 'types' and extents of worker participation, research and development, flexibility for reallocation of resources within the organisations between high and low 'productivity' sectors, communications and knowledge of the work process by decision-makers, 'restrictive' union practices and so forth may well, other things being equal, determine levels of output. If this is the case, such variables should be included in the right hand side of the function given above. The productivity of managerial skills, alternative participation schemes, is quite meaningful, though measurement (classificatory) problems may well impose on the actual compilation of such partial measures of productivity.

Stocks and flows

Our mention of the input of labour and capital has been in terms of the services these inputs provide. Both labour and capital are not purchased by the organisation for their own

2.

sake, but for the expected flow of services they will generate. For example, an establishment may purchase the services of a stock of 60 workers in a particular year – say between 9.00am and 5.00pm for five days a week. However, whilst the stock of labour may be constant from (working) day to day (excluding absences) the flow of labour services may vary as labour puts in more 'effort' over a particular period, or is more fully utilised etc. Similarly, a given stock of physical capital (machines) may remain constant over a particular period of time, yet the flow of services provided may vary if the capital is not being utilised at a constant level. The question we must put is whether we should be concerned with the (partial) productivity of a **stock** or **flow** of capital or labour?

The answer depends on the purpose for which the measures are derived. If our purpose is to explain the (relative) contribution labour or capital has made to generating a flow of output we must look to the services labour and capital provide, for it is from such services that output stems. However, relating the flow of output to the stock of labour serves a particular, and even unique, function. Economists are interested in the income generated by each employee for this provides the basis for an indicator (albeit not perfect) of changes in the standard of living. As we shall identify in Chapter 2 changes in per capita income are related to changes in output per employee, the relationship being also affected by changes in the relative prices of goods purchased to goods produced (imports and exports at the national level) and changes in the ratio of the working population to the population as a whole. Thus, relating the flow of output to the stock of labour input (number of employees) is, for this purpose, of particular interest.

Total input/factor productivity measures

Partial measures of productivity serve particular purposes and may be useful when the flow of output is related to what is considered to be a 'key' or scarce input. However, it is necessary to bear in mind that such measures do not, and cannot, tell the whole story. The main problem arises when partial measures of productivity are utilised as proxy indicators for 'efficiency'.

Consider two establishments each producing the same quantities of the same product, the first using capital intensive, the second labour intensive, modes of production.

Labour productivity (labour input being measured in flow or stock terms) will be greater for the first establishment simply because the 'productive powers' of labour have been increased owing to the greater 'aid' capital is providing. However, this is not to say the first establishment must be more 'efficient' than the second. Interest and depreciation charges will be higher for the first establishment. If cost minimisation is equated with 'efficiency' recourse has to be made to the relative prices of capital and labour (amongst other factors) before any judgement can be made. Similarly, the second establishment will yield higher capital productivity measures (capital being measured in stock or flow terms). Yet this establishment has higher labour costs to meet and again recourse must be made to the relative prices of capital and labour if we are to generalise about a company's relative performance.

Alternatively, the two establishments may employ the same ratios of capital to labour. Yet the first establishment may produce a given level of output from a smaller input of raw materials. For example, in a tailoring firm greater labour time may be directed to cutting in order to minimise waste. Partial measures of capital and/or labour productivity would not reflect the extra effort brought to bear by labour in the first establishment, yet for cost minimisation purposes it is certainly more efficient.

At first sight the problem may be resolved by compiling a series of all relevant partial productivity measures. Let us assume our concern lies with productivity changes over time for a particular organisation. Changes in capital, labour, energy and material productivity may all be identified. Yet we have no indication of the relative contribution of each of the inputs. We may note that as labour is directed to saving waste in bought-in cloth, cloth productivity increases by, say, ten per cent. However, since labour services are now, to a greater extent, concerned with cutting cloth the productivity of labour (unlike the case above) may fall by, say, five per cent. Such measures provide no indication as to whether the fall in labour productivity of five per cent is at least balanced by the increase in cloth productivity of ten per cent. Our discussion thus leads to the need for a measure of **total** (input or factor) productivity which in turn suggests the need for some aggregation procedure to combine the partial measures of productivity. We will return to this aggregation problem later and consider now some further features of the productivity relationships.

An alternative formulation to the relationship between the flow of output from, and inputs to, a production process may be given by (ignoring land):

$$O = f(K, L) \qquad \qquad \ldots(2)$$

where

$$O = (Q - (X_1 + X_2 \ldots X_n)$$

The reader may be concerned as to why inputs of materials/ services have been omitted from the right-hand side of the expression (as compared with expression (1) above). Such inputs have in fact been subtracted from the left-hand side of the expression. Net output is given by O which is the value of goods/services produced minus the value of bought-in goods and services required by the production process [1]. The production function given by (2) above relates net output to the input of capital and labour services, henceforth referred to as the **factors** of production.

The use of net output based production functions have arisen in a number of contexts and are worth discussing for they have a bearing on understanding the meaning and measurement of productivity. In National Accounting estimates of the output or production of the economy are based on net output. In aggregating the 'production' of different establishments double-counting is avoided. The output of one establishment, say car lights, when bought-in by another establishment, a car manufacturer, is not double-counted when net output is utilised, but would be included in the gross output of both establishments. In a closed economy the gross outputs of 'final' goods is approximately equal to the net output of the economy since no inputs enter the economy aside from 'free' air, sunshine, minerals (excluding extraction) and so forth. In an open economy imports become bought-in goods. Thus, one source of estimates of UK total production (or Gross Domestic Product) is the aggregation of net output for individual organisations [2]. Inputs of labour and the (value of the) stock of capital employed may be related to net output to provide separate partial measures of labour and capital productivity. At the level of the firm or plant a similar analysis can be employed. However, it should be apparent that when comparing estimates of, for example, labour productivity for two car manufacturers it is necessary to ensure that the use of gross or net output is consistently used.

If measuring changes in net output based productivity measures **over time** such measures incorporate changes in output and 'work done' on bought-in materials and services. For example, 20 employees in period 1 may be responsible for £60 thousand worth of gross output. In period 2, with the same length of working week, price of output, capital, wage rate, etc, this may remain at £60 thousand worth of **gross** output. However, employees in period 2 may be responsible for 'finishing' purchased raw materials when in period 1 they bought in already 'finished' raw materials. Thus, costs of bought-in materials in periods 1 and 2 might be £10 thousand and £7.5 thousand respectively. Labour productivity in any sense of the word has increased, yet the ratio of gross output to number of employees would remain constant (at £60,000/20 = £3,000). If net output is used to measure production the value of raw materials purchased is lower in period 2, reflecting the value of the additional work done in finishing the raw materials. As such labour productivity measures relating number of employees to **net** output for periods 1 and 2 respectively would be (£60,000-£10,000)/20 = £2,500 and (£60,000-£7,500)/20 = £2,625, thus reflecting the increase in work done by the same sized labour force and, thus, labour productivity.

Whilst the use of net output based productivity measures (as for example proposed by Smith, 1980 [3]) appear from the above discussion to be most appropriate, they suffer from a number of problems. The first is that they do not distinguish between changes in the relative prices and the volume of goods produced/used — though this will be discussed in further detail later. Second, the underlying production function behind such a relationship is highly restrictive and does not allow the (inter-related) impact of varying usage or work done on raw materials to be separately identified. The artificial process of shifting, through subtraction, bought-in inputs to the left-hand side of the production function is thus not necessarily valid. If the relative price of, say, material inputs to labour changes and this induces substitution between materials and labour in order to save materials, then material inputs, with its interaction with labour input, becomes an important variable in explaining output. To move bought-in (or intermediate) inputs to the left-hand side of the function via subtraction is to obscure the interaction between labour and capital (primary) inputs and bought-in (intermediate) inputs which together may explain production changes. Technically, the absence of any interaction effect is known as separability. Needless to say, if intermediate inputs are a stable function of gross output then gross or net output may be related to capital and labour services for a stable production function since variations in intermediate inputs give rise to no disturbing effects on the relationship between capital, labour and output.

The precise conditions for the use of net output on the left hand side of the production function, as opposed to gross output, are given by Bruno [4] and require that each intermediate input satisfies one of the following conditions:

> "(1) these inputs are used in fixed proportions to gross outputs, or
> (2) relative prices of intermediate inputs remain constant, or
> (3) the original gross-output production function is functionally separable into the intermediate and all primary inputs."[4]

Expression (2) also omits land from the right-hand side, as compared with expression (1). Land is, of course, an important input in agriculture and forestry and in studies relating to these sectors should be separately specified. In the manufacturing sector it is not so important or its contribution more stable and, for convenience, we will subsume it in the capital category of "other buildings and works", although in the United Kingdom national accounts the valuation of such structures exclude the value of the land which they occupy.

Functional forms and substitutability

We noted that the use of expression (2) imposed restrictions on the substitutability of the input of raw materials, energy and other bought-in goods and services with regard to capital and labour. The mathematical form the production function takes represents the technological relationship between the inputs and output. Whilst the right-hand side of expression (2) did not specify this form (we only said it was 'a function of' the left-hand side) in subtracting one from the other we imposed a sepcific and restrictive relationship. This relationship precluded any interaction between X_1, X_2 ... X_n and K and L and, in particular, inferred that one would not be substituted for the other.

Now, if gross output is our measure of output and all inputs are on the right-hand side of the equation the mathematical nature of the functional form should replicate the characteristics of the manner in which the inputs combine in practice in the production process. A firm may use n inputs to produce m outputs. The mathematical form of the production function describes the technological limits on the way the firm can act on the inputs to produce the required bundle of m outputs. The firm will be influenced by physical laws in which, say, chemical inputs react in a particular stage of the production of the output, the technological features of the capital equipment and physical limitations of labour in the way it can operate with, and substitute for, capital. Legal constraints (such as safety standards), information limitations, managerial 'capacity', flexibility of operation of labour all dictate the manner in which the inputs to the production process (including capital and labour) combine to yield the outputs and this influences the form of the mathematical function depicting such relationships. Choice between forms in estimating such functions depends on a priori assumptions as to characteristics of the relationships and econometric investigation [5].

The mathematical form of the production function has some bearing on the proposed framework and thus merits further consideration. We will assume that energy, material and other inputs are separable from capital and labour, solely to make the expressions less complicated. Needless to say, the same principles apply if we were to consider all inputs as separate variables in a gross output production function. It is interesting to note that most econometric studies of the production function used net output, and, given the substitutability arising from the not insignificant variations in oil prices, are prone to bias.

In 1928 Charles Cobb and Paul Douglas published the results of a study which related (using the econometric technique of multiple regression) aggregate inputs of capital and labour to aggregate net output from the US economy [6]. The technique of regression analysis requires one to specify a mathematical form by which changes in the values of a number of (explanatory) variables – capital and labour in this case – influence changes in a single (dependent) variable of interest – in this case, net output. Given data on the dependent variable and explanatory variables over a given time period (or across regions or industries) the 'features' of the relationship can be estimated using this technique. Such features are incorporated to a large extent in the 'coefficients' or elasticities of the function, which describe important characteristics of the relationship between output and inputs. The functional form used by Cobb and Douglas was:

$$O = A L^\alpha K^\beta \qquad \qquad \ldots(3)$$

where α and β are the elasticities of output with respect to labour and capital services input respectively. If labour input increases by x per cent (where x is very small) net output is to be expected to increase by αx per cent. Similarly, if capital input increases by x per cent (where x is very small) net output is to be expected to increase by βx per cent. Note that if $\alpha + \beta = 1$ this implies constant returns to scale, i.e., a change of x% in L and K will lead to a change of x% in O. The values of α and β can be derived for an economy/industry/firm/plant given data on O, L and K through the technique of multiple regression. If we stay with the Cobb-Douglas form we can derive some further features which may enhance our understanding of productivity.

The elasticities of output with respect to labour and capital allow us to determine the **marginal product** (or **marginal productivity**) of labour and capital. The marginal products of output with respect to labour and capital are derived by differential calculus. The very small increase in output resulting from a very small increase in labour input, capital being held constant, denoted by: $\partial O/\partial L$, is the marginal product of labour and a similarly defined $\partial O/\partial K$ is the marginal product of capital. Such values are not constant but vary according to the actual proportions in which labour to output and capital to output respectively are employed. Thus, if:

$$O = A L^\alpha K^\beta ,$$ i.e. a Cobb-Douglas production function,

the marginal product of labour is given by:

$$\frac{\partial O}{\partial L} = A \alpha L^{\alpha-1} K^\beta = \alpha \frac{O}{L} \qquad \ldots(4)$$

The marginal product of capital is given by:

$$\frac{\partial O}{\partial K} = A \beta L^\alpha K^{\beta-1} = \beta \frac{O}{K} \qquad \ldots(5)$$

Labour elasticity of output is:

$$\frac{\partial O}{O} \div \frac{\partial L}{L} = \frac{\partial O}{\partial L} \div \frac{O}{L} = \alpha \frac{O}{L} \div \frac{O}{L} = \alpha \qquad \ldots (6)$$

Capital elasticity of output is:

$$\frac{\partial O}{O} \div \frac{\partial K}{K} = \frac{\partial O}{\partial K} \div \frac{O}{K} = \beta \frac{O}{K} \div \frac{O}{K} = \beta \qquad \ldots (7)$$

The Cobb-Douglas form of the production function is, however, highly restrictive in that it implies that the elasticities of substitution are unity [7]. The Constant Elasticity of Substitution (CES) production function proposed in 1961 by Arrow et al [8] required the elasticities of substitution to be constant, but not necessarily equal to unity. However, since the early 1970s a new set of flexible functional forms have been developed which place no a priori restriction on the elasticities of substitution. These include the generalised Leontief function, the transcendental logarithmic (translog) form, the generalised Cobb-Douglas and the generalised Box-Cox forms. This latter functional form is so general it takes all preceding forms as special cases. Flexible functional forms possess the characteristic of being second-order approximations to arbitrary production functions [9].

The specification of functional forms can be identified as being important, since they have implications as to the actual nature of the production relationships required of productivity measures. We have seen this take one form in our discussion of net output based measures. For partial average productivity measures the main implication of the use of net output is that we cannot discern the separate relationship between material productivity and the factor of interest all being subsumed under one ratio. However, as we shall see in Chapter 2, such descriptive measures based on net output do have some virtues.

A second implication arises from the econometric studies of productivity based on the technique of multiple regression whereby α and β are estimated from a series of data on output, capital and labour. Such methods enable the marginal productivities of inputs with respect to outputs to be derived. Furthermore, hypotheses relating to constancy (or otherwise) of returns to scale, forms of technical change and estimates of the demand for factors at particular relative prices may be discerned [10]. Now all such studies require an initial specification of the form of the production function and the highly restrictive Cobb–Douglas form endemic in earlier (and in some later [11]) studies is but one of the criticisms launched against such studies [12].

A final implication is discussed in Chapter 3 where an alternative approach to the econometric framework for calculating partial and total productivity measures is considered. Implicit in this alternative index–number based approach is the choice of functional form and the above discussion should prove helpful in this context.

The 'neo-classical' framework

The marginal products of capital and labour are important in 'neo–classical' economic theory for they are held to determine the price of (or rewards to) capital and labour. In deciding whether to change the ratios by which capital and labour are employed a firm may look to the additional output resulting from additional inputs of capital and labour respectively. A machine (unit of capital) may be twice as expensive as a 'unit' of labour, however, an additional 'unit' of capital (similar machine) may generate four times the output of an additional unit of labour. Thus in determining factor proportions it makes sense (assuming cost minimisation to be coterminous with sense) to take account of the relationship between the relative price of capital and labour and their respective relative marginal products. It will be shown that under certain assumptions (including perfect competition, constant returns to scale, $\alpha + \beta = 1$ and the existence of no aggregation problems) that a cost minimising firm will equate the ratio of marginal products (the marginal rate of transformation) to factor price ratios. This is not to say that the marginal products and price ratios will be the only decision variables, the analysis resting on fairly restrictive assumptions.

The production function (assumed single–valued, continuous and, at least, twice differentiable) is given by:

$$O = F(K, L)$$

and the total cost (TC) function (excluding material and fuel costs) by: $TC = rK + wL$, where r and w are the price of capital and labour respectively.

The conditions for total cost minimisation and the input of K and L which will minimise total costs, for a given level of output, are determined from the Lagrangian:

$$L = rK + wL - \lambda[0 - F(K, L)] \qquad \qquad \ldots(8)$$

first order conditions are:

$$\frac{\partial L}{\partial K} = r + \lambda F_K = 0 \qquad \qquad \ldots(9)$$

$$\frac{\partial L}{\partial L} = w + \lambda F_L = 0 \qquad \qquad \ldots(10)$$

where F_L and F_K are the marginal products of labour and capital respectively. Thus:

$$\frac{F_L}{F_K} = \frac{w}{r} \qquad \qquad \ldots(11)$$

and

$$\frac{\partial L}{\partial \lambda} = 0, \quad \text{so} \quad 0 = F(K, L) \qquad \qquad \ldots(12)$$

Thus the optimal (cost minimising) solution occurs when the ratio of the marginal products of labour and capital (marginal rate of transformation) are equal to the ratio of factor prices.

For a Cobb–Douglas production function:

$$0 = A\, L^\alpha\, K^\beta \qquad \qquad \ldots(13)$$

we obtain:

$$\frac{F_L}{F_K} = \frac{\alpha}{\beta}\, \frac{K}{L} = \frac{w}{r} \qquad \qquad \ldots(14)$$

from which:

$$L = \frac{\alpha}{\beta}\, \frac{r}{w}\, K \qquad \qquad \ldots(15)$$

Substituting into the production function:

$$0 = AK^{(\alpha+\beta)} \left[\frac{\alpha}{\beta}\, \frac{r}{w} \right]^\alpha \qquad \qquad \ldots(16)$$

12.

which, after manipulating, provides the cost minimising input for capital, that is:

$$K = \left[\frac{O}{A}\right]^{\frac{1}{n}} \left[\frac{\alpha}{\beta} \ \frac{r}{w}\right]^{\frac{-\alpha}{n}} \qquad \dots(17)$$

where $n = \alpha + \beta$, representing the degree to which returns to scale operate and:

$$L = \left[\frac{O}{A}\right]^{\frac{1}{n}} \left[\frac{\beta}{\alpha} \ \frac{w}{r}\right]^{\frac{-\beta}{n}} \qquad \dots(18)$$

that is, the cost minimising input for labour.

The 'neo-classical' school in suggesting that marginal products explain the incomes accruing to capital and labour have, deservedly, aroused much criticism, though this will be discussed in Chapter 5. For the moment the reader should appreciate that the marginal product or productivity is an important and useful concept and differs from the previously noted partial average productivity concepts. The average productivity asks the historical question as to the output which has been generated by a flow of factor input. The marginal concept looks to the expected flow of output which is generated by a very small increase in a particular factor input, all other inputs remaining constant. A related concept is the **incremental** product of labour and capital which is similar to the marginal product but is not constrained to very small changes.

The equating of the marginal rate of transformation with relative prices for cost minimisation is also of interest, for when we face the problem of aggregating partial measures of productivity to derive total input/factor measures of productivity a basis for such aggregation is suggested by this theory. The theory thus provides a point of reference for discussing the validity of a particular aggregation procedure (discussed later in this chapter).

Having considered in further depth the production function framework we are now better placed to examine the meaning and measurement of total input/factor productivity. It was noted earlier that partial productivity measures each relate production changes to a specified input. As such, changes in each partial measure may have their origin in changes in other inputs. Labour productivity may be influenced by changes in the input of capital services, materials, energy, etc. Separate partial indices still provide a confusing scenario since whilst we may know, for example, that labour productivity and capital productivity have increased, whilst energy and material productivities have fallen, the combined effects of such flows on the organisation is not known. A given number of employees may produce more, but waste relatively more raw materials in doing so. Labour productivity increases and raw material productivity falls. Partial measures do not help us to discern whether the aggregate impact of such changes is in any sense favourable, and if so, by how much.

Total productivity provides an attempt to relate the aggregate impact of all inputs to output. If only factors of production are specified (in a net output production function) we are concerned with **total factor productivity**. If all inputs are considered (in a gross output function) we refer to the measure as **total input productivity**. It is the change in output having accounted for (or in econometric parlance) 'partialled out' the independent effects of all inputs. Consider again expression (3), the Cobb-Douglas production function.

The value of A in expression (3) is an indicator of the total factor productivity of the production process. Consider two establishments each employing the same inputs of capital and labour, all variables being measured in the same units. The establishment with the higher value of A will generate, for a given input of L and/or K a higher value of O and in this sense, be more 'efficient'.

Labour productivity, as a partial measure, becomes inadequate for it is dependent on the ratio of capital to labour. Labour productivity is given by:

$$\frac{O}{L} = A \frac{L^{\alpha}}{L} K^{\beta} = A L^{\alpha-1} K^{\beta}$$

$$= A^{-(1-\alpha)} K^{\beta}$$

$$= A \frac{K^{\beta}}{L^{(1-\alpha)}} \qquad \qquad \ldots (19)$$

For an establishment with constant returns to scale, namely $\alpha + \beta = 1$:

$$\frac{O}{L} = A \frac{K^{\beta}}{L^{(1-\alpha)}} = A \left[\frac{K}{L} \right]^{(1-\alpha)} \qquad \ldots (20)$$

The relationship between net output and labour input can only provide one part of the story, as Adam Smith noted, the growth in output can be increased only:

" ... by increasing either the number of its productive labourers or the productive powers of those labourers who had before been employed ... The productive powers of the same number of labourers cannot be increased, but in consequence either of some addition and improvement to those machines and instruments which facilitate and abridge labour; or of a more proper division and distribution of employment." [13]

The measurement of changes in total factor productivity may be derived from the production function (3), that is [14]:

$$A = \frac{O}{L^{\alpha} K^{\beta}} \qquad \qquad \ldots (21)$$

By taking logarithms of the variables and differentiating with respect to time:

$$\frac{\dot{A}}{A} = \frac{\dot{O}}{O} - \alpha \frac{\dot{L}}{L} - \beta \frac{\dot{K}}{K} \qquad \ldots (22)$$

where $\dfrac{\dot{A}}{A}$ represents very small rates of change in total

factor productivity and similarly for O, L and K; O, L and K are measures of real net output, real labour and capital services respectively (that is, with the effects of price changes excluded and measured by Divisia indices (see Jorgenson and Griliches, 1967 [15] and Chapters 2 and 3.

It is worth noting that changes in total factor productivity exclude from changes in real net output the effects of changes in real capital and labour services. In this sense total factor productivity has been deemed to be an almost 'costless' alteration in productive activity. Changes in labour productivity alone provided an inadequate indicator of productivity since they included the effects of changes in capital input, and capital productivity is inadequate owing to its inclusion of the effects of labour input. Total factor productivity excludes both such changes. The weighting allocated to changes in capital and labour input services respectively are given by β and α. In order that total factor productivity is associated with shifts in a production function, as opposed to movements along it, all marginal rates of transformation (ratios of marginal productivities) should be identified with price ratios (as identified in equation 11) for a production function with constant returns to scale. This leads to α and β respectively denoting the relative share of labour and capital in total net output, ($\alpha+\beta$ = 1). The use of prices to denote relative importance under assumptions of perfectly competitive markets and constant returns to scale provides a limitation on the analysis, since it must be confined to activities which are transacted in the market. Furthermore, all prices reflect private benefits and costs, divergences from social benefits and costs not being incorporated. However, this weighting problem will be considered later.

Our definition of total factor productivity has been such as to look to shifts in the production function not brought about by increases in the input of capital and labour services. However, we may define total factor productivity to suit our own purposes. Consider a factory which has for several years employed 50 perfectly maintained and fully utilised machines and 50 labourers, all homogenous, the organisation of the work process remaining unchanged. Should one machine be replaced, at the same real cost, by a more up-to-date machine incorporating technological developments, still manned by one person, net output will increase. If real capital input is measured by number of machines, the increase in net output stemming from technological progress will be incorporated in total factor productivity. Yet, if our indicator of capital input reflected the services provided by capital, no change in total factor productivity would ensue.

Changes in total factor productivity may arise from a reorganisation of the work process. Say a work study was bought-in to examine the organisation of the production process. Net output will decline as payments for services are made. Yet after the proposals are incorporated net output may rise over and above the fall in net output. Since inputs of capital and labour have remained the same total factor productivity will increase [16].

Consider a further example whereby the experience of the labour force increases and this results, on average, in a higher level of net output per employee for a given flow of capital services. By measuring the input of labour services in terms of number of employees the resulting increase in net output will be reflected in an increase in total factor productivity (upon re-estimating the function). Yet by giving greater weighting in the measure of labour services input to the more experienced workers with longer lengths of service the increase in net output may be subsumed in the indicator for increased labour input services.

From the above it may be apparent that the difficulties in measuring capital and labour services may result in facets of our inability to measure such inputs becoming incorporated into the shift parameter, A, that is, total factor productivity. Furthermore, the residual in any estimation instead of becoming an area of unexplained ignorance compounded with measurement error may be wrongly referred to as part of total factor productivity. It is not sufficient to say total factor productivity incorporates technological progress. It may well do. However, our aim should be to measure that part of technological progress embodied in machines as an input of capital services, for it is in this manner that growth in net output is 'explained'. If our purpose is to measure total factor productivity the 'variables' which contributed to it must be specified and justified on a priori grounds, as opposed to an inability to measure. It is on this very point that Jorgenson and Griliches's (1967) important contribution attacks previous studies and provides some empirical work for the US economy between 1945 and 1965. This study investigated the extent to which measured changes in total factor productivity were due to errors of measurement. As Jorgenson and Griliches note:

"Identification of measured growth in total factor productivity with embodied or disembodied technical change provides methods for measuring technical change,

17.

but provides no genuine explanation of the underlying changes in real output and input. Simply relabelling these changes as 'technical progress' or 'advance of knowledge' leaves the problem of explaining growth in total output unsolved." [17]

The problem thus becomes one of measurement in order to explain and it is for this reason that the second, fourth and fifth chapters of this book are devoted, in turn, to the problems of measuring real production, the real input of labour services and the real input of capital services. Meaning and measurement are inter-related for productivity measures in that it is for the user of the measure(s) to specify the inputs to be related to 'output'.

The proposed framework for this study is centred around the aim of fully accounting for changes in production. Changes in production may stem from a number of factors, including changes in labour and capital services. Variations in labour services may stem not only from variations in the stock of labour, but also from its 'effort', degree of utilisation, education and experience. Similarly, variations in the services provided by capital may stem from variations in the stock of capital, the effects of wear and tear, utilisation of capital and technological changes embodied in capital. Even with constant capital and labour services, economies of scale and reorganisation of the work process may well induce changes in production. In providing management with a detailed set of 'accounts' which seek to explain the sources of changes in production, management becomes better equipped to provide for future, beneficial, changes. Ideally, if every facet of every input could be properly specified and estimated from the stable production function the coefficients would yield the marginal products of each facet of the inputs. For example, the marginal product of a facet of the input of labour services, the marginal product of overtime work, may be compared with the price of overtime work relative to that of normal hours (including National Insurance, hiring costs, training, etc.) in order to establish whether paying for more overtime work is 'efficient' [18]. In practice estimation and aggregation problems will constrain such a detailed analysis. However, an 'accounting for growth' framework as outlined above is meaningful. Partial measures generally suffer from the problem of being influenced by other factors. Management, in decision making, are interested in identifying the sources of changes in production and, furthermore, influencing them.

The establishment of a financial incentive scheme is a management device to influence one facet of labour services input, that is, the 'effort' by labour. Our framework is simply an attempt to estimate factors which are implicit in managerial decision making. The approach has been considered, in a different context, by Griliches [19]:

"As I understand it, we are interested in "productivity" because we are interested in understanding the changes in output in the hope of uncovering the sources of our economic growth. We are interested in the forces that affect "output" because we hope, ultimately, to be able to affect them for the better. We approach this task first by trying to take into account the "obvious" factors: changes in labour and capital (and other materials if our measures are gross). We measure these factors as best we can, aggregate them using some sensible weighting procedure and get a "total input" index. We compare this index with our output index and call any discrepancy "productivity". Crudely speaking then, the "productivity" indexes measure those changes in input which have not been accounted for by the analyst's input measures. It is a measure of our ignorance of the unknown, and of the magnitude of the task that is still ahead of us."

However noble the above aim may be, in practice the task of fully and accurately accounting for growth will undoubtedly prove difficult, if not impossible. At the macro-level, especially for the United States, attempts to account for growth have grown in sophistication, a pioneer in this field being Edward F. Denison [20]. Yet, residual or unexplained variation remains in such studies – as would be expected considering the enormity and complexity of the task and the limited data available. Stone [21] proposed the use of adjustments based on direct estimation (given the variances so that output changes are fully 'accounted for' by inputs) and judgement. In a sense such a procedure may be more justified at the plant level. Management, in directing resources, implicitly make some judgement as to the marginal product of that resource (or facet of a resource). The decision to employ labour on overtime work implicitly requires a judgement as to the relative marginal product of overtime work and the relative price of such work. The determination of sources of changes in production by recourse to a framework which seeks to fully account for changes in production, whilst ambitious, is only seeking to put estimates, possibly previously made on a subjective basis, into a consistent and rigorous framework. Many of the problems existing at the macro level may well be avoided at the micro level given less aggregation problems, better data (at least potentially), a detailed knowledge of features of the production process and the possibility of controlling for variations in some variables. Yet given these advantages we may not fully account for growth. The task of 'whittling away' at the residual or unexplained variation though remains a valid exercise. If, for example, 80 per cent of variation in production is estimated to be 'explained' (in total) by variation in capital and labour services, the identification of the source of the remaining 20 per cent 'unexplained' variation is of interest. Is it economies of scale, improvements in the quality of material inputs not reflected in price, the result of a reorganisation of the work process following work study? Some of the answers may stem from broad guesstimates, as may the estimation of some components or facets of capital and labour service inputs.

The analysis, so far, has assumed the organisation to work effectively, management allocating resources to various areas as relative prices change with perfect knowledge of the organisation – like a well oiled machine. The complex organisation of establishments and many social factors which might influence motivation, response to pressures, require consideration. In the context of an organisation changes in morale, flexibility of employees, the social factors which lead to 'norms' in terms of effort and performance, the institutional systems which govern employee practices may well account for variations in output [22]. Flexibility in work practices, improved labour relations, greater commitment to the organisation and better morale may all be acknowledged as 'desirable' in the context of improving production from existing resources. Noting changes may be possible, assigning quantitative increases somewhat more difficult. Yet this is not to say the task should be ignored. Increases in production not arising from changes in quantifiable inputs can be isolated and linked to changes in work practices, morale. The very investigation of the source of such 'unexplained' variation may be quite fruitful at the level of the firm.

Aggregation problems

We consider two approaches to the analysis of changes in output with respect to inputs; the econometric and index

20.

number approach. In the first case marginal productivities with respect to output are derived for each input from the coefficients (elasticities) of a production function estimated by recourse to regression analysis. The functional form used represents the structure of the technological relationships between output and inputs and in the absence of any a priori indication of the form a strong case exists, as noted earlier, for the use of flexible functional forms. Developments in duality theory yield advantages in establishing the marginal productivities from the estimated cost functions (relating to input prices) as opposed to the equivalent production function (relating to input quantities) [23].

However, such analysis requires considerable econometric expertise which may not be available at the organisational level. Furthermore, such analysis provides an insensitive monitoring system for immediate changes in productivity arising from changes in the technological 'regime'. The addition of a new (present period) set of observations to an estimated production function will provide quite conservative tests of changes in the coefficients, though such stability tests do exist [24]. Only if the coefficients are stable (or the varying parameters can be appropriately modelled [25]) do econometric techniques provide the well defined indicators of marginal productivities based on sound and efficient criteria; yet such circumstances are not always the ones of interest. Econometric estimates do allow the inter-relationships between inputs to be analysed in terms of say, their substitutability and enable the estimated model, with some assumptions, to be formulated in terms of a wider organisational-wide model. Such possibilities are more limited in the second 'index number' approach which, however, provides an up-to-date monitoring system which can be readily and easily applied.

The index number approach monitors incremental changes in output and inputs and ratios thereof. Such measures do not efficiently utilise all data to derive estimates of marginal productivities, nor can they 'partial out' the effects of inter-related inputs. However, they can monitor the flows of each input with respect to output and ensure aggregation and representation as effectively as possible. Recent developments in the economic theory of index numbers show a unique correspondence between particular index number formulae and functional forms, as will be explained in Chapter 3. The process of chaining has received support from a number of approaches (e.g. the Divisia approach) and through its continual changing of the weights can go some way in accounting for changing coefficients (see Chapters 2 and 3). The need for index numbers arises for two reasons: first, to aggregate and measure changes in a range of items and qualities of items individually for raw material, energy, labour, capital and output; second, for the aggregation of the aggregate input indicators to account for output changes in the form of total factor/input measures. An account of the principles and use of such measures will be given in Chapters 2 and 3.

Whilst index numbers are concerned with aggregation within and between inputs and within outputs, a basis is required for the indication of the relative importance or 'weight' of inputs and outputs. The use of elasticities of inputs at the organisational level is impractical in the context of monitoring relationships which are hardly likely to remain stable. The equating of marginal products with input prices may not reflect reality. Shares of factor inputs may be utilised to represent output elasticities and constantly updated through the Divisia index in an attempt to offset aggregation errors (details are given in Chapters 2 and 3). Yet we are left with 'adding up' problems which the differential calculus and its concern with small changes obscures in studies of productivity over significant periods of time, or periods when changes in the technological relationships between inputs and outputs are taking place. Part of the problem lies with the nature of the exercise, that is the attempt to apportion out changes in output growth to changes in inputs. Whilst the calculus allows us to derive the contributions of individual inputs at the margin, allocating responsibility for output changes over periods of more significant change invites some criticism.

Furthermore, inputs do not always work in isolation, increases in output being greater than the sum of increases in individual inputs calculated one at a time, whilst holding all other inputs constant. Increases in one input may complement another, as for example, increases in the education of labour, capital and technological advance act both singularly and collectively to increase output, and to stimulate increases in each other. Education leads to technological advance and facilitates the use for more capital (by providing the necessary skills) as well as possibly increasing labour services from a given stock of labour. Nelson sums up the point well in considering the source of a well made cake:

"It is possible to list a number of inputs, flour, sugar, milk, etc. It is even possible to analyse the effects upon the cake of having a little bit more or less of one ingredient, holding the other ingredients constant. But it makes no sense to try and divide up the credit for a good cake to various inputs."

Our concern is that since each input has a price tag attached to it the decision to purchase inputs individually implicitly requires a knowledge of their relative contributions (for cost minimisation purposes) in order to produce a well made cake. It may make no sense to divide up the credit, yet we do so when prices are attached to inputs. If water can be substituted for milk, in using milk some idea of the relative contributions and relative prices of milk and water should enter the decision-making process. However, if milk's contribution influences not only the need for liquid, but complements other inputs to provide for texture, taste, lightness, etc., (as is more likely to be the case) considering milk as against milk substitute may be more reasonable. The lesson to be learned lies not with ignoring the exercise of accounting for production changes because of interaction effects, but isolating inputs and attempting to measure their contributions (for this is an implicit procedure in decision-making) bearing in mind that in some areas results for individual inputs may understate their real contribution in terms of interaction effects. Denison (1967 and subsequent studies [27]) employed the relative cost of each input for weights on the assumption that this corresponds to relative marginal products. Whilst we may question the equivalence of the relative prices/marginal products upon which this usage is based, suggestions for alternatives are difficult to come by. Shadow prices are one alternative, though these may be difficult to derive. Alternatively, we may say that whilst the equivalence may not be perfect at least, by chaining, changes in the relative prices (and hopefully marginal products) are included. It is interesting to note the practice in socialist countries where marginal productivity theory (of price/value) receives even less support than in the western world. At the macro-level productivity measures based on the labour theory of value are utilised. However, at the micro level:

"From a technical angle, there is no difference between the Kendrick total productivity (total factor/input) index and the similar, multifactor productivity and efficiency indices applied in the socialist countries. An important difference, primarily of the nature of interpretation, is, however, that in capitalist countries the joint weighting of labour and capital inputs are based on the theory of marginal productivity. This amounts to assuming that the proportions of wages and profits reflect the marginal productivities of the two kinds of inputs. Another difference how these calculations are used in analysis is the particular case when the contributions of labour and capital inputs to growth are separately shown on the basis of the respective marginal productivities." (Roman, 1982 : 55) [28].

Whilst the labour theory of value precludes the conception of the 'contribution of capital' the rationale for the weighting system based on relative prices (costs) thus appears to lie elsewhere, most likely with expediency. This is unlike the measures used at the macro level in socialist countries with capital being treated as embodied labour.

The basis of the weighting system utilised will be the relative costs of the inputs employed. However, since our purpose is to reflect changes in the contribution of each input to output we advise 'adjustment' to such costs arising from a knowledge of the organisation's characteristics. For example, if relative raw material costs rise in one period due to a temporary shortage as opposed to usage and no change in the productivity of raw material usage arises owing to these price changes, prices of raw materials may be allowed to increase at the same 'general' level as other inputs for the purpose of weighting calculations.

Terms-of-trade and price changes

So far the discussion has been in terms of isolating the physical contribution of capital and labour to changes in physical production (or real net output). Whilst productivity frameworks are often proposed in real or physical terms [29], the specification of such relationships in terms of ratios of money values is not unknown [30]. The problem with a ratio of, say, gross output to labour costs as a partial measure of labour productivity measured in money values (or current prices) is that changes in the ratio are not only determined by changes in the physical input of labour with respect to the physical quantity of goods produced, but also the relative price of labour to goods produced. Now such information may well be useful for the relative prices of, say, material inputs to outputs, labour remuneration to consumer goods, investment goods to retained profits (via outputs) provide for the terms-of-trade of the organisation, employees and investment respectively. However, a rigorous framework should, aside from isolating the physical contribution of factor inputs to outputs, enable the effects of relative prices to be demonstrated. The need to account for price and quantity effects has been appreciated by Eilon, Gold and Soesan; Gold; and Siegel [31]. This book incorporates such effects into its framework.

THE PROPOSED FRAMEWORK

The framework is illustrated by reference to the simplified data set given in Table 1 for two commodities over three years. Whilst some of the patterns of output and prices may be directly established from this data set this is only due to the limited number of cases considered. A firm with, say, 50 products and 20 (possibly different) raw material inputs requires the data to be aggregated if overall patterns are to be discerned. The principles outlined apply to any number of products over any number of years, months, weeks or days. To further simplify the illustration we consider only inputs of aggregate capital and labour services and raw materials assuming no energy inputs. We further assume that the inputs for capital and labour services stem from sub-accounts monitored and utilised for production management purposes and broken down, say for labour, to include adjustment for labour utilisation, skill mix, experience, sex, man-hours worked, 'seasonal' fluctuations and so forth. Considering the flow of such services with and without the adjustments allows the effects of such variables to be monitored. The framework outlined can, of course, be developed into a computer system without undue difficulties.

The principles behind and details of the formulae by which the information given here are calculated remain the subject of subsequent chapters. The purposes of this simplified example is to provide a context for understanding developments in further chapters.

Table 2 is a Basic Decomposition Table (BDT) which, by use of the chained Tornqvist index (see Chapters 2 and 3) decomposes value **changes** for all products and inputs into their respective aggregate price and quantity components. Such a table is useful in its own right as it allows us to

Table 1

Data Set on Output and Capital and Labour Services and Raw Material Inputs

		Product 1			Product 2		
		Price £'s	Quantity 000's	Value £000's	Price £'s	Quantity 000's	Value £000's
Output	1981	2	40	80	1.5	20	30
	1982	3	40	120	2	15	30
	1983	2.4	50	120	2	20	40
Inputs							
Capital:	1981	2,000	0.01	20	500	0.02	10
	1982	2,200	0.012	26.4	550	0.015	8.25
	1983	2,420	0.012	29.04	600	0.02	12
Labour:	1981	5,000	0.008	40	5,000	0.002	10
	1982	6,500	0.007	45.5	6,500	0.0015	9.75
	1983	7,000	0.008	56	7,000	0.003	21
Raw materials:	1981	100	0.1	10	5	0.6	3
	1982	110	0.1	11	6	0.45	2.7
	1983	180	0.09	16.2	12	0.45	5.4

Table 2
Basic Decomposition
1981 = 100

INPUTS

	OUTPUT			CAPITAL			LABOUR			RAW MATERIALS			TOTAL INPUT*		
	P	Q	V	P	Q	V	P	Q	V	P	Q	V	P	Q	V
81:	100.0	100.0	100.0	100.0	100.0	100.0	100.0	100.0	100.0	100.0	100.0	100.0	100.0	100.0	100.0
82:	146.0	93.6	136.4	110.0	105.1	115.5	130.0	85.0	110.5	112.1	94.0	105.4	120.6	92.4	111.4
83:	122.8	118.7	145.5	120.7	113.5	136.8	140.0	110.6	154.0	192.1	86.7	166.2	141.6	106.6	150.2

* Weighted sum of changes in inputs using the chained Tornqvist formula – in practice a matrix of weights would facilitate calculations.

P = unit value (price)
Q = quantity
V = value

identify, for example, that of the increase in the value of output between 1981 and 1983 for **all** products of 45.5%, 18.7% stemmed from changes in quantities produced and 22.8% from price changes. Note P x Q = V and ΔP x ΔQ = ΔV (1.228 x 118.7 = 145.5) – any disparities are due to rounding. The product of price and quantity changes equalling value changes is known as the 'factor reversal property' being met by Fisher's 'ideal' index and the Tornqvist index, both suitable for this system, the latter being applied in this illustration. The Laspeyres index, for example, does not possess this property.

Table 3
Partial and Total Input Productivity Indices in Money Terms, 1981 = 100

	Ratio of output to:			
	Capital	Labour	Raw Materials	Total inputs*
1981	100.0	100.0	100.0	100.0 (84.5)
1982	118.1	123.4	129.4	122.4
1983	106.4	94.5	87.5	96.9

* Equal to the value of capital, labour and raw materials which may sum to less than the value of output, the difference being gross profits. In 1981 inputs made up 84.5% of output value; figures in subsequent years relative to 100.0.

Table 3 shows changes in the ratios of the value of gross output to each input and total inputs in money terms (partial and total input money indices). The latter of course shows movements in gross profits, though the source of such movements in terms of physical quantities or relative prices is the subject of Tables 4 and 5 respectively. Thus, having noted that, for example, the productivity of capital in money terms increased by 18.1% between 1981 and 1982 (Table 3), we can establish from Table 4 that the physical or technological relationship between output and capital input actually fell by 10.9% with more capital being required per unit of output.

The increase in the productivity of capital in money terms stemmed from the 32.7% (Table 5) increase in the price of output relative to capital inputs. The system in enabling relative price movements (terms-of-trade) between outputs and inputs (or extended to form a matrix between all inputs) to be identified, provides a basis for decisions as to the substitution between inputs (for example, types of raw materials, capital, labour, or between labour and raw materials in attention given to 'waste saving'). However, as Table 5 shows in this illustration, favourable terms-of-trade changes in one period need not continue into the next.

Table 4
Partial and Total Input Producitivity Indices in Real Terms,
1981 = 100

Ratio of output to:

	Capital	Labour	Raw Materials	Total inputs
1981	100.0	100.0	100.0	100.0
1982	89.1	110.1	99.6	101.3
1983	104.6	107.3	136.9	111.4

Changes in total input productivity in money terms (aggregated across inputs) shows (Table 3) an increase of 22.4% between 1981 and 1982 and a fall of 3.1% in 1983 (compared with 1981 - or 20.8% compared with 1982). This increase in the profitability of the company for 1982/81 can be identified as stemming from only a small improvement (1.3%) in the (weighted) physical inputs/output ratio (Table 4) and a substantial increase (21.1%) in the price of outputs relative to the weighted combination of inputs. The subsequent fall of 20.8% in profitability, 1983/82, can be identified as deriving from a 9.97% increase in the technological efficiency or usage of (weighted) inputs relative to output and a 28.4% fall in the terms-of-trade of output relative to all inputs. We reiterate the often misunderstood multiplicative nature of the relationship between price and quantity changes to derive value changes.

With rounding errors the 1983 value relative to a common base of 1982 = 1.00 are V : 0.792;   Q : 1.0997;   P : 0.716.   Thus, 0.716 (1.0997) ≃ 0.792 all relative to a base of 1.00.

Table 5
Partial and Total Input (Unit Value) Terms-of-Trade Indices,
1981 = 100

Ratio of output to:

	Capital	Labour	Raw Materials	Total inputs
1981	100.0	100.0	100.0	100.0
1982	132.7	112.3	130.2	121.1
1983	101.7	87.7	63.9	86.7

Table 5 was concerned with changes in input prices relative to output prices since this affects income accruing to the organisation.   If, for example, the prices of equipment, raw materials or labour increase at a slower rate than the prices of goods produced, this represents a favourable movement in the organisation's terms-of-trade.   However, we might in addition be interested in the terms-of-trade of the employees.   Changes in the 'price' of labour or average wage rate may be compared with changes in the goods and services purchased by labour (best encapsulated for the UK in the All Items Retail Price Index) to monitor changes in the real purchasing power of labour remunerations.   Money values of labour remuneration may well, for example, increase though if the prices of goods consumed increase at a faster rate there is a fall in real purchasing power.   Table 6 shows the relevant details for our illustrations;   note that this analysis could be disaggregated by meaningful groupings of employees.

Table 6
Wages, RPI and Real Purchasing Power (1981 = 100)

	Labour remuneration (costs), value	RPI*	Real purchasing power
1981	100.0	100.0	100.0
1982	123.4	108.6	113.6
1983	94.5	114.0	82.9

* Assumed to be 5% for 1983 — note:
  (a) data available in the Department of Employment Gazette (monthly);
  (b) formula used for the RPI is the chained Laspeyres (Forsyth and Fowler, 1980).

Table 7 is the 'sources of growth' table and is derived from the volume of (real) input and output data in Table 4 coupled with value data for the weights in Table 1. The (weighted) percentage contributions could be arranged in a number of ways, but for this example we have used annual comparisons. Comparisons between 1983 and 1981 would, however, be quite easily derived. Table 7 shows that between 1982 and 1981 the 7.6% fall in total input was derived from a (weighted) combination of a 1.65% increase in capital input, a 8.20% fall in labour input and a 0.84% fall in material input. These figures are based on taking the annual increase in each input and apportioning to them a measure of their relative importance to the production process via the weighting system implicit in the Tornqvist formula. To say capital is increasing at x rate, and labour at y rate is limited in its usefulness if we do not know how important capital and labour is to the production process. Table 7 surmounts this problem. Note that output fell by 6.4% and the difference between this fall in output and the fall in total input is the measure of our ignorance. Some other factor has accounted for this relatively better showing for output than total inputs. Possibilities include a better organisation of the production process or economies of scale arising in 1982 not present in 1981. If technological improvements embodied in 'better' capital are not included in the measure of capital services then this might be a source. Note that the percentage contribution of individual inputs do aggregate to total input. For 1982 compared to a base of 1.00 for 1981 the increases in capital, labour and materials are, respectively, 1.0165, 0.918, 0.9916. The product of this (note we multiply) is 0.925, i.e. a fall from the base of 1.00 of 7.6% (with rounding errors). A similar analysis can be derived for 1983 compared with 1981.

Table 7
Sources of Growth

				Weighted percentage contribution		
	Capital	Labour	Raw materials	Total inputs	Output
1982/81	1.65	−8.20	−0.84	−7.60	−6.4
1983/82	8.00	19.02	−1.15	15.37	26.8

It is obviously not worthwhile discussing in detail the features of this data set, though the analytical power of this framework should be apparent as should its convenience as a computer system. All data for Tables 3, 4, 5 and 7 stem from the BDT given by Table 2. It remains, of course, only an analytical device keyed into quantitative indicators of a more complex reality. However, such indicators are efficiently and meaningfully combined to point the manager to some areas of concern and policy implications, or the more limited result of drawing attention to the end effect of more qualitative forces, the nature of which would require investigation.

[1]   Note this concept of net output differs from the more limited one employed in the UK censuses of production in which the inputs of services are not deducted.

[2]   Details of the measurement of production in the UK are given in Appendix I and Jackson, D A S, Introduction to Economics: Theory and Data, Macmillan, London, 1982, pp.67-82.

[3]   Smith, G, 'Planning for productivity', Long Range Planning, Vol.13, 1980.

[4]   See Bruno, M, 'Duality, Intermediate Inputs and Value-Added', and, for further details, Diewert, W E, 'Hick's Aggregation Theorem and the Existence of a Real Value-Added Function', both in Fuss, M and McFadden, D (editors), Production Economics: A Dual Approach to Theory and Applications, Volume 2, Applications of the Theory of Production, Contributions to Economic Analysis 111, North-Holland Publishing Co., Amsterdam, 1978, pp.3-16 and 17-43 respectively and Gollop, F M, 'Accounting for Intermediate Input: The Link between Sectoral and Aggregate Measures of Productivity Growth' in National (USA) Research Council, Measurement and Interpretation of Productivity, National Academy of Sciences, Washington D.C., 1979, pp.318-333.

[5]   For a detailed account see Fuss, M, McFadden, D and Mundlak, Y, 'A Survey of Functional Forms in the Economic Analysis of Production', in Fuss, M and McFadden, D (editors), Production Economics: A Dual Approach to Theory and Applications, Volume 1, The Theory of Production, Contributions to Economic Analysis 110, North-Holland Publishing Co., Amsterdam, 1978, pp.219-268.

[6]   Cobb, C and Douglas, P H, 'A theory of production', American Economic Review, Supplement to Vol.18, 1928, pp.139-165.

[7]   A very readable account of the properties of the Cobb-Douglas production function and the interpretation of its parameters is given in Pen, J, Income Distribution, Penguin, Harmondsworth, 1971, Chapter 4, pp.76-157 and pp.413-429. For a more mathematical, and

slightly more rigorous, account see Wallis, K F, Topics in Applied Econometrics, Lectures in Economics, 5, Gray-Mills Publishing Ltd, London, 1973.

[8] Arrow, K J, Chenery, H B, Minhas, B and Solow, R M, 'Capital labour substitution and economic efficiency, Review of Economics and Statistics, August 1961, pp.225-250; see also Berndt, E R, 'Reconciling Alternative Estimates of the Elasticity of Substitution, Review of Economics and Statistics, Vol.58, No.1, 1976, pp.59-68.

[9] For details see Berndt, E R and Khaled, M S, 'Parametric productivity measurement and choice among flexible functional forms', Journal of Political Economy, Vol.87, No.61, 1979, pp.1220-1245.

[10] See Wynn, R F and Holden, K, An Introduction to Applied Econometric Analysis, Macmillan, London and Basingstoke, 1974, Chapters 1 and 3.

[11] For example, Leslie, D G and Wise, J, 'The productivity of hours in UK manufacturing and production industries', Economic Journal, Vol.90, No.357, March 1980, pp.74-85.

[12] For criticisms of such studies see Ranadive, K R, Income Distribution: The Unsolved Puzzle, University Press, Oxford, 1978, pp.204-218, and a survey of such studies, Hahn, F H and Mathews, R C O, 'Growth and technical progress: a survey', Economic Journal, Vol.74, 1964, and Kennedy, C and Thirlwall, A P, 'Technical progress: a survey', Economic Journal, Vol.82, No.325, March 1972, pp.11-74.

[13] Smith, A, An Inquiry into the Nature and Causes of the Wealth of Nations, Edwin Cannan, 1904, Book 2, Chapter 2.

[14] For further details see Kennedy, C and Thirlwall, A P, 'Technical progress: a survey', Economic Journal, Vol.82, No.325, March 1972, and Kendrick, J W, Productivity Trends: Capital and Labour, National Bureau of Economic Research, Occasional Paper 53, NBER, New York, 1956, who originally fostered their use.

[15] See Jorgenson, D W and Griliches, Z, 'The explanation of productivity change', Review of Economic Studies,

Vol.34, 1967, pp.460-61.

[16] There may well be a time lag in the relationship - if payment was made in one period and proposals incorporated in a second, total factor productivity would be lower when estimated up to the end of the first year as compared with the estimation for up to the end of the second year - coefficients being assumed to remain stable.

[17] Jorgenson and Griliches, 1967, op.cit., p.250. Jorgenson and Griliches refer in the quote to a paper which reiterates this point, namely: Jorgenson, D, 'The Embodiment hypothesis', Journal of Political Economy, Vol.74, 1966.

[18] Leslie, D G and Wise, J, 'The productivity of hours in UK manufacturing and production industries', Economic Journal, Vol.90, No.357, March 1980, pp.74-85.

[19] Comment by Griliches, Z on paper by Creamer, D, 'An appraisal of long-term capital estimates: some reference notes', in Output, Input and Productivity Measurement, Conference on Research in Income and Wealth, Studies in Income and Wealth, Vol.25, National Bureau of Economic Research, 1961.

[20] Denison, E F, Accounting for Slower Economic Growth: The United States in the 1970s, Brookings Institution, Washington D.C., 1979. For more recent estimates see Denison, E F, 'The interruption of productivity growth in the United States', Economic Journal, Vol.93, No.369, March 1983, pp.56-78.

[21] Stone, R, 'Whittling away at the residual: some thoughts on Denison's growth accounting, a review article', Journal of Economic Literature, Vol. XVIII, 1980, pp.1539-1543.

[22] For an excellent survey in which such factors are stressed, see Nelson, R, 'Research on productivity growth and productivity differences: dead ends and new departures', Journal of Economic Literature, Vol. XIX, September 1981, pp.1029-1064.

[23] See Fuss and McFadden, 1978, op.cit.

[24] See Maddala, G S, Econometrics, McGraw-Hill, Kogakusha, Tokyo, Kogakusha, 1977.

[25] Details are given in Judge, G G, Griffiths, W E, Hill R C and Lee, T–C, The Theory and Practice of Econometrics, John Wiley & Sons, New York, 1980.

[26] Nelson, 1981, op.cit.

[27] Denison, E F (assisted by Poullier, J P), Why Growth Rates Differ: Postwar Experience in Nine Western Countries, Brookings Institution, Washington, 1967. See also Note 20.

[28] Roman, Z, Productivity and Economic Growth, Akademiai Kiado, Budapest, 1982.

[29] For example, Roll, Y and Sachish, A, 'Productivity measurement at the plant level', OMEGA, The International Journal of Management Science, Vol.9, No.1, 1981, pp.37–42.

[30] For example, Smith, G, 'Planning for productivity', Long Range Planning, Vol.13, 1980.

[31] Eilon, S, Gold, B and Soesan, J, Applied Productivity, Analysis for Industry, Pergamon Press, Oxford, 1976; Gold, B, Productivity, Technology and Capital, Lexington Books, Toronto, 1979; and Siegel, I H, 'Productivity measurement at the firm level: a brief survey', pp.9–30, in Adam, N R and Doyramaci, A, Productivity Analysis at the Organisational Level, Studies in Productivity Analysis III, Martinus Nijhoff Publishing, Boston, 1981.

2 The measurement of production

This chapter examines some of the measurement problems involved in the concept of "production". Many of the principles considered also relate to the measurement of 'bought-in goods and services' and, in particular, the input of materials. Much of the discussion will thus be concerned with the linkages between the output and material inputs to the organisation.

The word "production" has various meanings. The production of a textile factory, for example, could be said to be the number of square metres of cloth produced during a given period. But this measure of production does not indicate the amount of **work done** by the factory. Consider the example of a factory in the textile industry which buys in raw cotton, makes the cotton into yarn, and weaves the yarn into cloth, producing X square metres a year. Contrast this with a factory which buys in X square metres of cloth, dyes that cloth, and then sells X square metres of dyed cloth. Clearly, there is a sense in which the amount of "work done" in the former factory is much greater than in the latter factory, even though the "production" in terms of square metres of cloth is the same.

Furthermore, physical output as a measure of "production" does not take account of the difference between the **quality** of the two products (one being dyed cloth, the other being plain cloth); nor does it take into account the work done to achieve the improvement in quality. Finally, and most importantly, such a measure fails to take account of the extra work done in the cloth-making factory, arising from the yarn-spinning and cloth-weaving activity, none of which takes place in the cloth-dyeing factory. The problem of the difference in quality may be handled by treating the output from the two factories as two different products; namely, square metres of dyed cloth and square metres of plain cloth. However, for the measurement of production changes at the macro-level, distinguishing between all such products in this manner would be impractical.

There is even a further paradox. It is often not possible to compare production in physical units, such as square metres of cloth, with physical production of a different product, say number of shirts manufactured. So we tend often to use the sales value of output: that is, the sales receipts obtained from selling the volume of the flow of output. In this case, the sales value of the output from the cloth-dyeing factory would be **greater** than the sales value of the output from the cloth-making factory, and this difference would reflect (not necessarily accurately) the work done to achieve the quality difference. However, **less** "work" is done in the cloth-dyeing factory, in that it does not undertake the yarn-spinning and cloth-weaving activities, and this fact is not reflected in these measures of production. Therefore, the sales value of output may not be employed as a measure of aggregate production. Additionally, if we were to use the sales value of output as a measure of production, then the total production of the textile sector, in this example, would be the sales receipts of the cloth-making factory plus that of the cloth-dyeing factory. However, in a future period of time the two factories may merge, so rendering our measure of total production equal to the value of sales receipts of dyed-cloth only, although the amount of work done may have remained the same. The sales value of output may only be usefully employed as a measure of production if related, in the aggregate, to "final" products as they reach their end-use of consumption or investment. "Final demand" is a useful measure for the purpose of ascertaining the amount of saleable products produced for end use in an economy, but not for the purpose of measuring productivity at the organisational level, for which purpose we need a measure of production which relates to the amount of work done.

There is a solution to these measurement problems. That

solution is to measure "output" in terms of the sales value of what is produced **minus** the cost of the bought-in materials used to produce the output. This is similar to net output, though relates (initially) to sales value rather than value of goods produced. Adjustments will be subsequently introduced. This measure of output is known as **value added** because it measures the value which is added to the materials which are bought-in.

In the example we have been considering, it can be seen that the value added produced by the yarn-spinning and cloth-weaving factory is likely to be much greater than the value added produced by the cloth-dyeing factory, because the cost of bought-in materials in the former factory will be much lower than in the latter.

Value added is thus closely related to the amount of work done in an enterprise, and is therefore closely related to the amount of factors of production required. Because value added is measured in monetary units, it is comparable across different industries, and may therefore be aggregated over industries.

Furthermore, it is from the flow of value added produced by an enterprise that payments are made for the services of factors of production such as labour and capital and to meet the needs of the state, for example taxes.

Therefore, a useful measure of production, when considering productivity, is value added. With the recent development of value-added accounts [1] financial incentive schemes based on value added [2] and the advocation of value added as an organisational objective [3], the use of value added as a basis for productivity measures may be supported in the interests of developing a consistent information system. It is because of the popularity of the concept [4] that attention will be given to its use in the measurement of production. However, in spite of the clear manner in which it accounts for changes in the ratio of bought-in inputs to outputs to better represent 'work done' it is **not** most suited for our framework.

We note that by using a measure based on output only, such as sales value, two firms which produce the same quantity of end products may give identical production figures. We are concerned that if the two firms undertake different amounts of work in previous stages of the production process this will not be reflected by a measure of production based on sales value or the value of production. Yet the use of value added (or net output) is but one way of dealing with the problem since in its simple subtractive procedure it assumes a specific (separable) form of relationship between the inputs used. This is particularly restrictive in econometric work. Furthermore, the subtractive process in its attempt to represent changes in the material input to output relationship serves to obscure the actual changes taking place. By separately specifying such input and output changes the proposed framework reveals the changing relationships. As labour is diverted to, say, 'finishing' material inputs rather than purchasing 'ready-finished' inputs, labour productivity will fall (output remaining constant), material productivity will increase with (hopefully) the net effect of total input productivity increasing. As noted above, some attention will, however, be devoted to the measurement of production from a value added/net output approach given the popularity of value added based information systems (see Appendix II). Such a discussion will also provide a useful basis for deriving the principles for measuring gross output and material input for the purpose of our proposed framework based on gross output as an indicator of aggregate production.

There are two main problems concerned with the measurement of production. The first concerns the treatment of inventories. The second concerns the adjustment of the money measure of production to allow for price inflation.

INVENTORIES AND STOCK APPRECIATION

We have said that production may be measured by the flow of sales receipts during a given period and bought-in inputs by the cost of bought-in materials during a period. This is an oversimplification. Apart from the fact that we must include not only bought-in materials, but also all other bought-in services, there is the problem of inventories of materials, work-in-progress, and finished products (a) taken over from the preceding period, and (b) handed on to the next period.

Consider the measurement of production. An enterprise may not sell all its output during the year, but may build up its inventories of finished and semi-finished products. Because its sales during the year may thus be lower, we cannot allow this situation to result in a smaller flow of production for the purpose of productivity measurement since inputs of labour, capital etc have been employed in this productive effort. The solution to this problem is to treat such inventories handed over to the succeeding period as a sale. Then it does not matter if the enterprise sells less in the market during the specific year but builds up its inventories instead, because these inventories will be counted as a sale in the calculation of production.

Consider the measurement of material inputs. An enterprise may start the year with a large inventory of materials. During the given year it may wish to use this inventory without fully replacing it. The enterprise may, therefore, not buy-in materials during the year under consideration. This cannot be allowed to mean that its cost of materials during that year is thereby smaller for the purposes of productivity measurement. Productivity is concerned with the technological relationships between inputs usage and output. The solution to this problem is to treat inventories taken over from the preceding period as a purchase of materials, etc. Then it does not matter if the enterprise buys less materials in the market during the specific year but uses its inventories instead, because the latter use will be deducted as a purchase of materials in the calculation of the cost of material inputs.

Thus, the complete formula for measuring 'gross output' is:

receipts from sales during the year
plus
value of semi-finished and finished goods at the end of the year
less
value of semi-finished and finished goods at the beginning of the year

The formula for measuring the cost of inputs is:

cost of bought-in goods and services at the beginning of the year
plus
value of inventories of materials etc at the beginning of the year
less
value of inventories of materials etc at the end of the year

Net output is gross output less the cost of bought-in goods and services. Value added differs from net output for our purposes in that the latter has allowances made for changes in inventories, whilst the former does not.

However, this solution – treating inventories taken over from the preceding period as a purchase and inventories handed over to the succeeding period as a sale – involves a difficult problem of valuation because in such a "purchase" and such a "sale" no money actually changes hands. Therefore, a valuation has to be imputed to the items in the inventories: that is to say, those items have to be valued at some prices. One accounting practice is to value items in the inventories at the prices more or less currently ruling at the time the valuation is made.

This practice causes a serious difficulty if the prices used for these valuations change. Let us consider the case when prices used to value items in the inventory all double during the year. Table 2.1 illustrates the problem with some imaginary numbers. In year 0 an enterprise starts off with a certain volume of inventories, valued in terms of prices ruling at the beginning of the year, at 100 (thousand pounds – as with figures hereafter for this section). We will assume that all inventories are of semi-finished and finished goods though the principles equally apply to inventories of materials etc. During the year it sells 400 worth of goods to buyers. The enterprise ends year 0 with the same volume of inventories valued, in terms of prices ruling at the end of the year, at 100 because prices are assumed not to have changed during the year.

Table 2.1

Illustration of stock appreciation and the calculation of gross output

		£ thousands	
	Year 0	Year 1(a)	Alternative treatment Year 1(a)
(1) Valuation of inventories taken over from preceding period	100 (b)	100 (b)	200 (d)(e)
(2) Receipts from sales	400	400	400
(3) Valuation of inventories handed over to succeeding period	100 (c)	200 (d)	200 (d)
(4) Gross output: (2) + (3) − (1)	400	500	400
(5) Stock appreciation	−	−	100 (e)

(a) All volumes remaining the same as in Year 0.

(b) Valued at prices ruling at beginning of Year.

(c) Valued at prices ruling at end of Year 0: prices assumed to remain unchanged during year.

(d) Valued at prices ruling at end of Year 1: prices assumed to have doubled during Year 1.

(e) In this example, stock appreciation ("stock" here means inventories of finished and semi-finished goods) is the difference between opening inventories valued at closing prices and opening inventories valued at opening prices (see first row); stock appreciation is positive if prices are rising and negative if prices are falling.

If we apply the previously-given formula for calculating gross output during Year 0, we have:

gross output = 400 + 100 - 100

= 400

In Year 1, the enterprise starts off with inventories valued, in terms of prices ruling at the beginning of the year, at 100. during the year it sells to buyers the same volume of output for 400. However, just before the end of the year, prices for the valuation of items in the inventory double, so that the same volume of inventories, valued in terms of prices ruling at the end of the year, is now 200.

If we apply the formula for calculating gross output during Year 1 to those figures we would have:

gross output = 400 + 200 - 100

= 500

Clearly something is not right: the "work done" by the enterprise during Year 1 is exactly the same as that done during Year 0 and the inventory volumes are the same, yet gross output is much larger.

The solution to this problem is to adjust the valuation of inventories to allow for price changes. The simplest solution is to value the opening inventories in terms of prices ruling at the end of the year. Because all prices are assumed to have doubled, opening inventories will be valued at 200 and gross output will now be equal to 400; as it was in Year 0 when the volume of work done was the same. We note that the firm's income may increase in Year 1; but our concern is with physical relationships in productivity measurement.

The difference between the valuations of opening inventories valued in terms of prices ruling at the end of the year and of opening inventories valued in terms of prices ruling at the beginning of the year, is known as "stock appreciation" (in Britain) or "inventory valuation adjustment" (in the United States).

There is, however, a difference between theory and practice in the measurement of stock appreciation in the British national accounts. The national accounts statisticians note that:

"the valuation of total stocks held at the beginning and

end of the period of account for national and sector balance sheets should **theoretically** be made at replacement prices"; [5]

that is, at the prices ruling at the end of the period. However, in practice,

"the method adopted in the United Kingdom — similar methods are used in other countries facing the same statistical problem — is to revalue the accounting figures of **both** opening and closing stocks, by the use of price indices, at the **average** market prices of the period. The difference between the revalued opening and closing stocks is then treated as the net investment in stocks at current (i.e. constant) prices for national accounting purposes".[6]

Finally,

"the difference between investment in stocks, or the value of the change in the physical quantity of the stocks, measured in this way, and the value of the change in stocks shown by the accounting data, is the amount of stock appreciation, which may be positive or negative". [7]

In terms of our example, and now assuming that prices increase at a steady rate throughout the year so that the price index at the beginning, middle and end of Year 1 is, respectively, 1.00, 1.50, and 2.00, the UK Central Statistical Office procedure means that both opening and closing stocks are revalued approximately as follows:

$$\text{opening stocks to} \quad 100 \times \frac{1.50}{1.00} = 150$$

$$\text{and closing stocks to} \quad 200 \times \frac{1.50}{1.00} = 150$$

This shows zero investment in stocks (more precisely referred to as the value of the change in the physical quantity of stocks), and this is correct under the assumptions of this example. The difference between, on the one hand, closing minus opening stocks as valued by the accountants (from the middle column in Table 2.1: namely, 200 **minus** 100 = 100) and, on the other hand, the (zero) investment in stocks, is stock appreciation; to wit, 100. To enlarge the illustration, suppose that closing stocks had increased by 10 per cent in volume terms while prices had doubled: closing stocks would then have an accounting valuation of 220; and the CSO procedure would revalue opening stocks to 150 (as before) and closing stocks to:

$$165 \left[= 220 \quad x \quad \frac{1.50}{2.00} \right] ,$$

so measuring investment in stocks as 15 (which, be it noted, is half-way between investment in stocks of 10 as would be measured at constant opening prices, and investment in stocks of 20 as would be measured at constant closing prices); in turn, this would measure stock appreciation as 105 (**equal to** (220-100) -15). In terms of economics, this can presumably be interpreted as comprising appreciation of 100 on opening stocks and of 5 due to the increase in the volume of stocks.

For the purpose of productivity measurement, it is essential that stock appreciation be excluded from measures of gross output and the cost of material inputs in real terms, though the terms-of-trade effects may be incorporated in the respective account.

Deducting stock appreciation from annual flow of gross output allows for changes in prices which occur during the year itself. What about price changes which occur from one year to the next? It is clearly possible for work done to remain the same each year, and for the inputs or the factors of production also to remain the same, while the money measure of gross output rises because prices rise. But this rise in money gross output relative to inputs or factors of production does not mean that productivity has risen. Therefore we need to allow for the effect of rising prices over the course of several years.

Our concern at this stage should be with the measurement of changes in gross output after allowances have been made for the effects of price changes, or to use the correct terminology, our concern is with the **deflation** of gross output. However, a number of concepts are tied up with this procedure which may be best illustrated by considering the deflation of net output. The deflation of gross output and cost of bought-in goods etc. can then be separately identified. Instead of subtracting these components (as in measures of net output), their ratio may be taken to allow us to identify changes in the partial productivity of materials. The examination of the deflation of net output may also be useful in itself, since, as noted earlier, the use of net output/value added based systems are receiving some attention.

THE DEFLATION OF NET OUTPUT

Net output is calculated as the difference between the money value of sales receipts from selling a quantity of output and the money flow of costs from buying a quantity of material etc. inputs. In both cases allowances are made for changes in inventories and stock appreciation is deducted. When measuring productivity we are concerned only with the changes which occur in net output as a result of changes in these quantities. We do not wish to consider changes occurring as a result of price changes. The necessity for such price adjustment is universally accepted. In the light of this, any vagueness about just how such price adjustments should be made merits concern. We will start the discussion by considering the deflation of value added. Adjustments for stock changes will be incorporated later to form measures of net output.

The method generally adopted is simply to adjust value added by the change in the sale price per unit of whatever it is that is being produced. For example, if in the cloth-dyeing enterprise the sales price of dyed cloth per square metre had risen by 25 per cent between Year 0 and Year 1, then it is common to "deflate" value added by dividing the money flow of value added in Year 1 by 1.25.

We need to be quite clear that this commonly-used method is a theoretically unsatisfactory way of allowing for price inflation. Its unsatisfactoriness can be shown by example (A) given in Table 2.2 and again relating to our illustrative cloth-dyeing factory. During Year 0, the cloth-dyeing factory buys in 1,000 square metres of plain cloth at a price of £1 per square metre and sells 1,000 square metres of dyed cloth at a sales price of £2 per square metre. Assuming for simplicity that the enterprise carries no inventories, its value added in Year 0 is the difference between the receipts from sales and the cost of bought-in materials; that is, value added **equals** £2,000 **minus** £1,000 **equals** £1,000.

During Year 1 the quantity of bought-in materials and the quantity of coloured cloth sold are exactly the same as in Year 0: the "work done" by the cloth-dyeing factory has not changed. But during Year 1, in example (A), the sales price of coloured cloth rises by 25 per cent to £2.50 per square

47.

Table 2.2
The effect of price changes upon value added

	m² per annum	Price per m²	Current price value of quantity, £	Price index Year 0 = 1.00	Constant price value of quantity, £
Year 0					
Materials	1,000	1.00	1,000	1.00	1,000
Sales	1,000	2.00	2,000	1.00	2,000
Value added	-	-	1,000	-	1,000
(A) Year 1: usual method					
Materials	1,000	1.00	1,000	-	-
Sales	1,000	2.50	2,500	-	-
Value added	-	-	1,500	1.25 (a)	1,200
(B) Year 1: deflating sales					
Materials	1,000	1.00	1,000	-	1,000
Sales	1,000	2.50	2,500	1.25	2,000
Value added	-	-	1,500	-	1,000
(C) Year 1: deflating sales					
Materials	1,000	1.20	1,200	-	1,200
Sales	1,000	2.50	2,500	1.25	2,000
Value added	-	-	1,300	-	800
(D) Year 1: double-deflation					
Materials	1,000	1.20	1,200	1.20	1,000
Sales	1,000	2.50	2,500	1.25	2,000
Value added	-	-	1,300	-	1,000
(E) Year 1: usual method					
Materials	1,000	1.25	1,250	-	1,000
Sales	1,000	2.50	2,500	-	2,000
Value added	-	-	1,250	1.25	1,000

(a) Sales price index

metre. Without allowing for this inflation it appears that
value added has risen to £1,500.

The work done during Year 1 has not changed by comparison
with Year 0, so it is clearly necessary to adjust the money
flow of value added. The sale price of output has risen by 25
per cent: that is, £2.50 (the sale price in Year 1) **divided
by** £2.00 (the sale price in Year 0) equals 1.25. However, if
we divide the "money" value added of £1,500 by 1.25 to
"deflate" it to base-year prices – example (A) – we find that
the resulting "real" value added is £1,200, which is still
bigger than the £1,000 of Year 0, although the work done has
not altered.

Clearly, this example (A) shows that deflating value added
by the change in the sale price of output does **not** adjust
properly for inflation. If we deflated the money value of the
flow of sales receipts, rather than the flow of value added –
example (B) – then the money value of sales receipts
(deflated) becomes £2,500 **divided by** 1.25 **equals** £2,000, and
value added, in price adjusted terms, is £1,000, just as it
was in Year 0. Therefore, the change in the sale price of the
goods sold ought to be used to deflate the money value **of
sales receipts** if we are to get a satisfactory adjustment to
value added which removes the effect of inflation.

However, example (C) shows that this adjustment by itself
may give misleading results. Example (C) shows a case where
the sale price of goods sold has risen to £2.50, and the
purchase price of materials bought-in has risen to £1.20. If
we simply deflated the money value of sales receipts but still
took the money value of materials at £1,200, then value added
in Year 1 would appear to have fallen to £2,000 **minus** £1,200
equals £800 by comparison with £1,000 in Year 0.

Clearly, this is a "wrong" answer because the work done has
remained the same. However, if we **also** deflate the total cost
of materials by the proportionate rise in the purchase price
of materials, which is 20 per cent – that is: £1.20 **divided
by** £1.00 **equals** 1.20 – the money value of the inputs is
reduced to £1,000 – example (D) – and value added, in price
adjusted terms, is again £1,000, which is the right answer.

Example (A) showed that we got an inappropriate answer if we
deflated value added itself by a price index for goods sold:
the price deflator must be applied to the value of sales as
shown by example (B). Example (C) showed that this method

gives an inappropriate answer if the price of material inputs is changing too. The cost of materials must also be deflated by a price index relating to the change in the price of materials – example (D).

Deflating value added by an index of the price of goods sold will give the "right" answer only if the price of material inputs **and** the price of goods sold have both increased by the same proportion. This is shown by example (E) where both input and output prices have risen by 25 per cent, and where the latter is used to deflate value added·as in example (A). The assumption of identical price movements is therefore the implicit assumption behind the use of an index of sale price to deflate value added. But we seldom know whether such an assumption is justified.

The only method guaranteed to give the "right" answer is to deflate **both** sales receipts **and** materials cost, each by their respective price movements. This method of calculating price-adjusted value added to eliminate the effects of inflation is known as the method of double-deflation. When considering changes in productivity over a period of time, it is essential to use the method of double-deflation for the calculation of "real", or price-adjusted, value added.

To use the method of double-deflation, it is necessary to have the following information:
   (1) the flow of sales receipts;
   (2) the cost of materials;
   (3) the prices of goods sold;
   (4) the prices of materials bought.

In practice, of course, enterprises often produce more than one product and generally use more than one input. This means that data needs to be collected on all (or most) of the quantities of items produced and on their prices, and likewise for material inputs.

If the data gathered is sufficiently detailed, the money value of each particular item sold and the money cost of each particular material used can be separately deflated by its own price change, and the "real" values so estimated can then be added together.

If the data is insufficiently detailed then information should be collected on the main items and separate price indices calculated (a) for goods sold and (b) for materials used.

The method of double—deflation therefore provides the only suitable measure of the "real" value of what is **produced**. But it may not provide a suitable measure of real **income**. In general, economists are conditioned to thinking of value added – production or output – as coterminous with income. And in current prices it always is. But when adjusting for inflation, there is a way in which movements in "real" income may diverge significantly from movements in "real" output. This fact has been recognised in the adjustment of the domestic prduct to allow for changes in the terms of (foreign) trade. We may imagine a country producing year in and year out the same volume of goods and services, a constant volume of which are exported and importing other goods and services. Suppose now that the price index for imports increases relative to the price index for exports. Although the domestic production of value added, and the volume of exports, remains unchanged, the country is able to enjoy less consumption and/or investment because the volume of imports remains unchanged while its costs have increased relative to what is recouped from the sales of exports. (We are supposing that there is no accumulation of foreign debts or running down of foreign exchange reserves.) That is to say, while the country's real output has remained the same, its real income has diminished, due to the adverse movements in the terms—of—trade – the ratio between the export price index and the import price index. The adjustment – that is, diminution – of the constant real product for adverse changes in the terms—of—trade, so as to obtain the (smaller) real national income is effected quite simply

> "and consists in replacing the estimate of the exports of goods and services at constant prices by the current value of exports deflated by the price index of all imports and purchases abroad of goods and services". [8]

The question of "real" price—adjusted income differing from "real" price—adjusted output is a complex issue and needs further explanation. Suppose, as before, that in Year 0 the cloth—dyeing factory buys and uses 1,000 square metres of plain cloth at a price of £1 per square metre, and produces and sells 1,000 square metres of dyed cloth at a price of £2 per square metre – as shown in Table 2.3. Suppose also that value added is divided between labour and capital with the total wage bill being £700 and the surplus being £300.

Table 2.3

The divergence between "real" output and "real" income

	m² per annum	Price per m²	Current price value of quantity, £	Price index Year 0 = 1.00	Constant price value of quantity, £
Year 0					
Materials	1,000	1.00	1,000	1.00	1,000
Sales	1,000	2.00	2,000	–	2,000
Value added	–	–	1,000	–	1,000
Wages	–	–	700	–	700
Surplus	–	–	300	–	300
(F) Year 1: double deflation					
Materials	1,000	1.40	1,400	1.40	1,000
Sales	1,000	2.50	2,500	1.25	2,000
Value added	–	–	1,100	–	1,000
Wages	–	–	800	–	700 ?
Surplus	–	–	300	–	300 ?
(G) Year 1: consumer price deflation					
Materials	1,000	1.40	1,400	–	–
Sales	1,000	2.50	2,500	–	–
Value added	–	–	1,100	–	880
Wages	–	–	800	1.25	640
Surplus	–	–	300	1.25	240

In Year 1, the price of materials inputs rises to £1.40 per square metre, a rise of 40 per cent, and the price of output rises to £2.50 a square metre, a rise of 25 per cent. Current-price value added now becomes £1,100. We may assume that the workers obtain all of the extra value added, so the wage bill rises to £800 and the surplus stays at £300. Applying the method of double-deflation (example (F) in Table 2.3) causes the constant-price estimate of value added still to be £1,000; and this is appropriate because the amount of work done has remained unchanged.

However, the question now arises as to how we should divide this constant-price value added (indicating the unchanged amount of work done) between labour and capital. Indeed, it may be asked whether it is sensible to do this at all. One could say that the division of value added remained in the same ratio as in Year 0, and that therefore the constant-price value of wages was £700 and the constant-price value of the surplus was £300 - example (F). Although this sounds paradoxical, it is nevertheless meaningful, but it means only that the use of factors of production has remained the same. The problem is that when we think of real **income** we are interested not in whether the volume of factor services put into work done has altered or remained the same, but in whether the volume of purchases which can be made out of a given money income has altered or remained the same; that is, we are concerned not with work done or with factor services used, but with the **benefit** in terms of consumption out of that income.

We can illustrate this by supposing that the workers and the capitalists consume only dyed cloth. Then the benefit resulting from money income is the volume of dyed cloth that can be purchased with income. In Year 0, the workers and capitalists in the cloth-dyeing sector can consume 500 square metres of cloth (their combined income divided by the price of cloth): the workers can consume 350 square metres and the capitalists 150 square metres. The workers and capitalists in the rest of the economy consume the remaining 500 square metres. In Year 1, the workers and capitalists engaged in cloth dyeing can consume between them only 440 square metres of cloth (£1,100 **divided by** £2.50) and the workers and capitalists elsewhere can consume the remaining 560 square metres. The real income of those engaged in cloth dyeing has fallen because cloth consumption has been diverted away from them to others in the economy: this is the result of the change in the "terms of trade" between the cloth-dyeing sector of the economy and the other sectors of the economy; that is to say, the change (decline) in the ratio of the output price to the input price.

The consumption of those engaged in cloth dyeing has fallen to 88 per cent of its former level: from 500 square metres to 440 square metres. This means that their combined money income in Year 0 of £1,000 must now have a "real", price-adjusted, value of £880. We may obtain this result if we deflate their incomes by the output price index as shown in example (G). The workers' real income in Year 1 is £640 and the capitalists' real income is £240, making a total real income of £880, which is 88 per cent of income in Year 0. Although we have worked this example in terms of cloth consumption and the price index for dyed cloth, the same result applies if a general consumer price index is used and if the movement in that price index differs from the movements in the input and the output price. It is only when all price indices change by exactly the same amount that there will be no divergence between double-deflated "real" output and consumer price deflated "real" income.

The method of deflating factor incomes by a consumer price index is appropriate when measuring changes in the **benefits** derivable from income, but it does not give the answer appropriate to the question concerning the amount of **work done** (except in special and coincidental circumstances). The method of double-deflation is appropriate when measuring changes in real output, but will not serve the purpose of showing what is happening to real incomes. This problem seems to be an issue behind the criticisms of the method of double-deflation [9], but it is not a valid objection to double-deflation to say that it will not indicate changes in real income — it is not meant to.

If we intend to relate the measure of real value added to the productive use of the factors of labour and capital, then the method of double-deflation is the correct method. The choice of which method of deflation to use, therefore, depends on the purpose to which the measure is to be put.

In our discussion of the measurement of value added, we have noted the need to take account of the effects of changes in the prices both of outputs and of inputs. In the example of the cloth-dyeing factory, this can be achieved by measuring value added in Year 1 at the prices of Year 0. In general terms, for k and j inputs, the annual flow of double-deflated value added may be measured for a comparison between period T, a current period, and period 0, a fixed base period, by:

$$\sum_{i=1}^{k} P_{i0}Q_{iT} \quad - \quad \sum_{h=1}^{j} p_{h0}q_{hT} \qquad \ldots (1)$$

where

P	=	price per unit of output sold
p	=	price per unit of inputs purchased
Q	=	quantity (number of units) of output sold per annum
q	=	quantity (number of units) of inputs purchased per annum
0	=	subscript denoting fixed base year
T	=	subscript denoting current year
i	=	subscript denoting different outputs, 1 to k
h	=	subscript denoting different inputs, 1 to j.

One question which arises in connection with this expression concerns the problem of inventories. Expression (1) obviously applies if there are no opening or closing stocks, but how does the formula apply in the presence of stocks, and changing stocks at that? In order to incorporate stocks into the formula we may denote quantities of opening stocks in Year T by a superscript prime Q'_T and q'_T, for outputs and inputs respectively; quantities of closing stocks by a superscript double-prime, Q''_T and q''_T; and the closing price of Year 0 by P''_0 and p''_0 for outputs and inputs respectively. We then have a modified form of (1) for the calculation of net output at constant prices:

$$\sum_{i=1}^{k} P_{i0}Q_{iT} \quad - \quad \sum_{h=1}^{j} p_{h0}q_{hT}$$

$$+ \sum_{i=1}^{k} P''_{i0}Q''_{iT} \quad + \quad \sum_{h=1}^{j} p''_{h0}q''_{hT}$$

$$- \sum_{i=1}^{k} P''_{i0}Q'_{iT} \quad - \quad \sum_{h=1}^{j} p''_{h0}q'_{hT} \qquad \ldots (2)$$

Obviously, expression (2) is more than a little cumbersome, but it is the only correct formula. However, it may be manipulated into something more amenable by noting that we have, in effect, the changes in stocks measured at closing prices:

$$\sum_{i=1}^{k} P_{io}Q_{iT} - \sum_{h=1}^{j} P_{ho}q_{hT}$$

$$+ \sum_{i=1}^{k} P''_{io}(Q''_{iT} - Q'_{iT})$$

$$- \sum_{h=1}^{j} P''_{ho}(q'_{hT} - q''_{hT}) \qquad \ldots (3)$$

These changes in the stocks of finished goods (including work in progress and in the stock of materials, all valued at closing prices, can then be subsumed into the flow variables proper. That is, the Q_{iT} can then be taken to include the stock changes, $(Q''_{iT} - Q'_{iT})$ because these changes are now annual flows. Likewise, the q_{hT} can be taken to include $(q'_{hT} - q''_{hT})$ — note the change in order — and both of these stock change variables can be assumed to be valued at the appropriate prices. So we may revert to the "simple" expression (1), but only on the understanding that the value of output and input includes stock changes, in the way shown in expression (3).

On this understanding, net output produced during period T, measured at prices ruling in period 0 — as given by expression (1) — may be compared with net output produced during period 0. This comparison shows, in index form, the relative change in value added between period 0 and period T measured at constant prices of the base period 0. The expression, shown below, is the Laspeyres index of double—deflated net output:

$$\left[\frac{\displaystyle\sum_{i=1}^{k} P_{io}Q_{iT} - \sum_{h=1}^{j} P_{ho}q_{hT}}{\displaystyle\sum_{i=1}^{k} P_{io}Q_{io} - \sum_{h=1}^{j} P_{ho}q_{ho}} \right] \qquad \ldots (4)$$

In practice, however, the numerator in expression (4) is not usually calculated by multiplying each of the i outputs and each of the j inputs (in the current period) by their respective prices in the base period, summing and subtracting from the total flow of current output valued at base-period prices, the total flow of inputs valued at base-period prices.

The more common practice is to compile a single index for all the i output prices (1 to k) and another single index for all the h input prices (1 to j). These price indices are then used, respectively, to deflate the current value of gross output and the current cost of inputs. The advantage of this procedure is that if sufficiently detailed price information is not available for all outputs or inputs, the respective value figures can be deflated by price indices compiled from available data. Such a procedure is recommended since assumptions of equal price changes are generally more plausible than equal production changes. The result is again a measure of double-deflated net output at constant prices.

However, to achieve this measure of double-deflated net output at constant **base period** prices, the appropriate form of price index must be used. These appropriate price indices are Paasche, or current weighted, price indices.

For this purpose, the "correct" method of calculating the output price index is to relate the total gross output in period T to what the value of the quantity of goods produced during period T would be if the prices of period 0 were then to be charged. An exactly similar method applies to the price index for all inputs. If we omit the subscripts over which summation takes place, the Paasche price index for output is given for a comparison between periods 0 and T with the base period = 1.00, by:

$$\frac{\Sigma P_T Q_T}{\Sigma P_0 Q_T} \qquad \ldots (5)$$

(In all the following expressions we shall also omit the subscript denoting the products over which summation takes place unless this is required.)

The Paasche price index for inputs is likewise given by:

$$\frac{\Sigma p_T q_T}{\Sigma p_0 q_T} \qquad \ldots (6)$$

By dividing expression (5) into the current period's value of gross output and by dividing expression (6) into the current period's cost of all inputs, and by then subtracting the latter result from the former result, the total net output at constant base period prices is obtained.

That is:

$$\frac{\dfrac{\Sigma p_T Q_T}{\Sigma p_T Q_T}}{\dfrac{}{\Sigma p_0 Q_T}} \quad - \quad \frac{\dfrac{\Sigma p_T q_T}{\Sigma p_T q_T}}{\dfrac{}{\Sigma p_0 q_T}}$$

$$= \quad P_0 Q_T \quad - \quad P_0 q_T \qquad \ldots (7)$$

Or, writing (7) out in full:

	Gross output during period T	**divided by**	Paasche output price index (5)
minus	Cost of inputs during period T	**divided by**	Paasche input price index (6)
equals	Volume of output during period T valued at prices of period 0		
minus	Volume of input during period T valued at prices of period 0		

Therefore, as we stated, if a measure is wanted of double-deflated net output at constant base period prices, the correct price index formula is the Paasche price index.

We must now consider the general usefulness of such a measure of real net output at base period prices. Such a measure of real net output is, in essence, a Laspeyres, or base weighted, index of the volume of output, where "volume" is being measured as double-deflated net output.

The Laspeyres volume index is widely used, and is recommended by the United Nations [10]. The Laspeyres index is simpler to compute and easier to understand than many alternative formulae. Movements in the index answer the meaningful question: what would be the rate of change in "production" if prices were unchanged from the base year?

However, two major points should be noted. The first is that the Laspeyres index is, of course, base weighted; that is, it ascribes, as a measure of the relative "importance" to be given to changes in volume of outputs and inputs, the value of that output or input relative to the total value of output or input which exists in the base year. This may not always be desirable, especially if the relative importance of outputs or inputs is changing. Second, for positive value added at current prices, the Laspeyres measurement of double-deflated net output may occasionally give a negative result; this allegedly serious shortcoming is discussed in Silver and Golder [11].

An alternative index number formula for measuring real double-deflated net output is the Paasche index. The Paasche double-deflated net output index relates value added in the current period, T, to what net output in the base period would have been if measured at the prices ruling in the current period. This index is given for a comparison between period 0 and period T by the formula:

$$\frac{\Sigma p_T Q_T - \Sigma p_T q_T}{\Sigma p_T Q_0 - \Sigma p_T q_0} \qquad \ldots (8)$$

The denominator of expression (8) may be more readily calculated by multiplying a Laspeyres price index for output by the value of gross output in period 0, and by then deducting from this the product of a Laspeyres price index for inputs and the value of inputs in period 0.

The Laspeyres price index for output, comparing period T with period 0 with base period = 1.00, is given by:

$$\frac{\Sigma p_T Q_0}{\Sigma p_0 Q_0} \qquad \ldots (9)$$

The Laspeyres price for inputs is likewise given by:

$$\frac{\Sigma p_T q_0}{\Sigma p_0 q_0} \qquad \ldots (10)$$

The denominator of (8) may be calculated using price indices (9) and (10) as follows:

$$\left[\Sigma P_0 Q_0 \right] \left[\dfrac{\Sigma P_T Q_0}{\Sigma P_0 Q_0} \right] - \left[\Sigma P_0 q_0 \right] \left[\dfrac{\Sigma P_T q_0}{\Sigma P_0 q_0} \right]$$

$$= \Sigma P_T Q_0 - \Sigma P_T q_0 \qquad \qquad \ldots (11)$$

Or, writing (11) out in full:

	Gross output during period 0	**multiplied by**	Laspeyres output price index (9)
minus	Cost of inputs during period 0	**multiplied by**	Laspeyres input price index (10)

equals Volume of output during period 0 valued at prices of period T

minus Volume of input during period 0 valued at prices of period T

We should note that a Laspeyres price index should not be **divided** into net output measured at current prices, although this is an unfortunately common practice, due to the availability of Laspeyres price indices. The result of such a computation is:

$$\dfrac{\dfrac{\Sigma P_T Q_T}{\Sigma P_T Q_0}}{\Sigma P_0 Q_0} - \dfrac{\dfrac{\Sigma P_T q_T}{\Sigma P_T q_0}}{\Sigma P_0 q_0} \qquad \ldots (12)$$

It can be seen that, unlike (11), expression (12) has no obvious economic interpretation.

To summarise, if a series is wanted of double-deflated net output at base prices – a Laspeyres index of double-deflated net output – then the correct price index formula to use in deflating both output and the cost of inputs is the Paasche price index. If net output in the base period is required to be measured at current period prices – a Paasche index of double-deflated net output – then the correct price index formula to use in "multiplying up" gross output and the cost of inputs in the base period is the Laspeyres price index.

Having discussed two methods of measuring changes in real (double-deflated) net output, namely the Laspeyres method – expression (4) – and the Paasche method – expression (8) – we consider now another method. This index is known as the Divisia index, after its originator F Divisia [12]. The Divisia index has achieved a growing acceptance as a method of measuring changes in real output [13].

Net output during any period can be expressed as:

$$vV = \sum_{i=1}^{k} P_i Q_i - \sum_{h=1}^{j} P_h q_h \qquad \ldots (13)$$

where v denotes the "price" of a unit of net output and V denotes the "quantity" of net output produced. By differentiating both sides totally with respect to time and by then dividing through by vV, we may obtain the Divisia index of real double-deflated net output as follows:

$$\frac{dV}{V} = \sum_{i=1}^{k} \omega_i \frac{dQ_i}{Q_i} - \sum_{h=1}^{j} u_h \frac{dq_h}{q_h} \qquad \ldots (14)$$

where ω_i and u_h are the weights assigned to relative changes in outputs and inputs respectively. These weights are as follows:

$$\omega_i = \frac{P_i Q_i}{\sum P_i Q_i} \qquad \ldots (15)$$

$$u_h = \frac{P_h q_h}{\sum P_h q_h} \qquad \ldots (16)$$

As can be seen, the weights are the relative shares of the input value of the ith product in total output or the cost of the hth input in total input. A more detailed discussion and derivation is given in the next chapter.

It is, of course, not possible to calculate the exact form of the Divisia index, because this requires the measurement of changes in quantities of output and in quantities of inputs over infinitesimal periods of time. However, it is possible to calculate an approximate form of the Divisia index. This approximation is the chained index.

The Laspeyres and Paasche indices previously described are calculated using weights from only a single year. That is to say, these indices compare net output in one period directly with net output in another period, making an adjustment to remove the effects of price changes between the two periods. The chained index does not make such a direct comparison between two periods, but rather forms a series of "links" by comparing net output in period 1 with period 0, to form a first link, then by comparing period 2 with period 1, to form a second link and so on, until net output in period T is compared with net output in period T-1, to form the Tth link. In each "link comparison", adjustments are made to remove the effects of price changes. The index measuring the change in "real" net output between period 0 and period T is obtained by successive multiplication of all the intervening link terms.

The chained index thus continually adjusts (at discrete intervals) for changes in the relative importance of outputs and of inputs. The chained index is, therefore, an approximation to the Divisia index. But what formula should be used to calculate the change in real net output between each of the individual links?

As the length of the time period for each link comparison becomes shorter, so too does the difference between the results of the different formulae become smaller. For infinitesimal periods of time, all formulae yield the same result – namely, the Divisia index.

The chained Laspeyres index, for a measure of the change in real (double-deflated) net output between period 0 and period 2 is given with base period = 1.00, by the product of the Laspeyres index for period 0 and 1 and the Laspeyres index for period 1 and 2.

$$
\left[\frac{\dfrac{\Sigma\,P_1 Q_1}{\Sigma\,P_1 Q_1}}{\dfrac{\Sigma\,P_0 Q_1}{\Sigma\,P_0 Q_0}} \; - \; \frac{\dfrac{\Sigma\,P_1 q_1}{\Sigma\,P_1 q_1}}{\dfrac{\Sigma\,P_0 q_1}{\Sigma\,P_0 q_0}}\right]
$$

$$x \left[\cfrac{\dfrac{\dfrac{\sum P_2 Q_2}{\sum P_2 Q_2}}{\sum P_1 Q_2} - \dfrac{\dfrac{\sum P_2 q_2}{\sum P_2 q_2}}{\sum P_1 q_2}}{\sum P_1 Q_1 - \sum P_1 q_1} \right]$$

$$= \left[\frac{\sum P_0 Q_1 - \sum P_0 q_1}{\sum P_0 Q_0 - \sum P_0 q_0} \right] \times \left[\frac{\sum P_1 Q_2 - \sum P_1 q_2}{\sum P_1 Q_1 - \sum P_1 q_1} \right]$$

$$\ldots (17)$$

The chained Paasche index of real double-deflated net output may be similarly derived from (8) and (11) above:

$$\left[\cfrac{\sum P_1 Q_1 - \sum P_1 q_1}{\left[\sum P_0 Q_0\right]\left[\dfrac{\sum P_1 Q_0}{\sum P_0 Q_0}\right] - \left[\sum P_0 q_0\right]\left[\dfrac{\sum P_1 q_0}{\sum P_0 q_0}\right]} \right]$$

$$x \left[\cfrac{\sum P_2 Q_2 - \sum P_2 q_2}{\left[\sum P_1 Q_1\right]\left[\dfrac{\sum P_2 Q_1}{\sum P_1 Q_1}\right] - \left[\sum P_1 q_1\right]\left[\dfrac{\sum P_2 q_1}{\sum P_1 q_1}\right]} \right]$$

$$= \left[\frac{\sum P_1 Q_1 - \sum P_1 q_1}{\sum P_1 Q_0 - \sum P_1 q_0} \right] \times \left[\frac{\sum P_2 Q_2 - \sum P_2 q_2}{\sum P_2 Q_1 - \sum P_2 q_1} \right] \qquad \ldots (18)$$

As has already been stated, if the length of time within each link comparison is relatively small, the difference between the results of the chained Laspeyres, Paasche or any other formula will be small. However, if the lengths of time are long, and the differences correspondingly large, an appropriate formula to use in the chained index may be Fisher's "ideal index" [14].

The Laspeyres index uses as weights the relative importance of outputs and inputs in the "base", or first year, of each link; the Paasche formula takes its weights from the "current", or second year, of each link. As the geometric average of the Laspeyres and Paasche indices, Fisher's "ideal index" seems accordingly appropriate, though see Chapter 3 for further support on different grounds. This version would give the following as the chained index for real double-deflated net output between periods 0 and 2:

$$
\sqrt{\left[\frac{\Sigma P_0 Q_1 - \Sigma P_0 q_1}{\Sigma P_0 Q_0 - \Sigma P_0 q_0}\right] \times \left[\frac{\Sigma P_1 Q_1 - \Sigma P_1 q_1}{\Sigma P_1 Q_0 - \Sigma P_1 q_0}\right]}
$$

$$
\times \sqrt{\left[\frac{\Sigma P_1 Q_2 - \Sigma P_1 q_2}{\Sigma P_1 Q_1 - \Sigma P_1 q_1}\right] \times \left[\frac{\Sigma P_2 Q_2 - \Sigma P_2 q_2}{\Sigma P_2 Q_1 - \Sigma P_2 q_1}\right]}
$$

. . . (19)

However, the computation of (19) is a somewhat complicated matter. Thus it may be simpler to use the Laspeyres form — [17] — or the Paasche form — [18] — of the chained index.

It appears that the chained index is generally superior to the base weighted form for an index of industrial production (quantity index or double-deflated net output) [15]. As an instance of the possible extent of the divergence between the two, Table 2.4 shows a comparison between the base-weighted indices of production in Zambia for non-ferrous ores (including the production of refined copper) and for total manufacturing. In the case of non-ferrous ores, where the quantities and prices of the products tend approximately to remain in the same ratio to each other, the base-weighted and the chained indices move very closely together. But in the case of the far more heterogeneous groupings for all manufacturing industry, there is a considerable divergence between the base-weighted and the chained indices: by 1976,

seven years after the start of the indices, the chained index
has risen 11.5 per cent more than the base-weighted index.
Such divergences also affect the constituent components of
the indices as Table 2.5 shows, where the 1976 divergences
range from 15 to -18 per cent.

Differences of this magnitude are obviously matters of
concern when one is trying to assess such things as
productivity growth, and this illustration forcefully backs
up the argument for the importance of measuring real output
properly.

Table 2.4
Indices of industrial production in Zambia, 1969 = 100

Year	Non-ferrous ore (a)		Total manufacturing (b)	
	Base weighted	Chained index	Base weighted	Chained index
1969	100	100	100	100
1970	91.8	91.8	111.3	111.3
1971	85.4	85.4	121.0	122.5
1972	93.6	93.8	129.2	133.8
1973	91.8	92.0	132.0	142.2
1974	95.8	96.1	141.1	157.3
1975	86.8	86.9	136.3	150.0
1976 (c)	95.0	94.9	129.6	144.5
1977 (c)	88.5	88.7	127.3	136.4

(a) Including copper refineries; this index has a 1969 base
    weight of 79.8 per cent in the total index of industrial
    production (mining, manufacturing and electricity); the
    fall in production in 1970 and 1971 is largely accounted
    for by the Mufulira mine diaster of 25 September 1970,

when a large part of the Mufulira mine was flooded with mud and slurry, killing 89 men; in 1969, Mufulira accounted for 23 per cent of ore hoisted on Zambia's copperbelt.

(b) This index has a 1969 base weight of 16.7 per cent in the total index of industrial production.

(c) Provisional.

Source: Republic of Zambia, Central Statistical Officer: Monthly Digest of Statistics, November/December 1977, Tables 17(a) and 17(b), p.14; Monthly Digest of Statistics, March/June 1978, Tables 17(a) and 17(b), p.14 (Zambian data compiled by Dudley Jackson).

Table 2.5

Sub—sector indices of industrial production in Zambia

| Sub-sector | Index of industrial production in 1976 (a) 1969 = 100 | | Percentage divergence of chained index from base weighted index |
	Base weighted	Chained index	
Food, beverages and tobacco	132.7	152.6	15
Textiles and clothing	158.7	171.2	8
Wood and wood products	67.7	55.3	−18
Paper and paper products	155.4	173.3	12
Chemicals, rubber and plastic	130.6	149.0	14
Non-metallic mineral products	129.5	145.8	13
Basic metals (b)	100.3	90.8	−9
Metal products and others	122.9	135.0	10

(a) 1976 figures are provisional.

(b) Excluding copper refineries.

Source: Republic of Zambia, Central Statistical Office, Monthly Digest of Statistics, November/December 1977, Tables 17(a) and 17(b), p.14.

The Deflation of Gross Output

Having considered in some detail the deflation of net output, the principles involved in the deflation of gross output should be apparent. In addition, the deflation of bought-in inputs of materials has been considered. To derive double-deflated net output the deflated value of material inputs is subtracted from the deflated value of gross output. However, our framework outlined in Chapter 1 focussed on the deflation of gross output and material inputs separately to derive changes in the real volume of output and material input and the formation of partial indices of productivity by dividing the former by the latter. The choice of index number used has been argued to be important and some support has been given to a chained Fisher's ideal index (though a suitable alternative is the chained Tornqvist index). However, this subject requires further clarification and will be covered in Chapter 3.

The previous discussion of double-deflated net output has also served to emphasise the difference between isolating changes in real income and output. It should be apparent that to derive changes in the real purchasing power of earnings changes in earnings should be deflated by changes in the Retail Price Index. Such an index provides an indicator of changes in the prices of an 'average' bundle of goods. By deflating earnings by the Retail Price Index an indicator of changes in the benefits or purchasing power of earnings is derived.

Thus, for the purpose of the framework outlined in Chapter 1 the previous discussion warns us to take account of stock changes, deduct stock appreciation and to deflate gross output and the input of materials to form the quantity (Q) column in the Basic Decomposition Table (2, Chapter 1) for output and raw materials. These columns form the basic data for calculating the partial productivity index for materials in real terms given by Table 4. Once the volume or real input has been derived for output and materials the price component can be realised by recourse to the identity that changes in value are equal to changes in the price component multiplied by the real (volume) component and Table 5 (Chapter 1) ensues. Table 6 (Chapter 1) shows changes in real purchasing power as considered above.

Other Considerations

Having considered the measurement of production in some detail, several points remain to be made. First, we have utilised the relative prices of goods produced/bought-in as indicators of the relative importance of such goods. Relative prices reflect private costs/returns as opposed to social costs/returns. Thus, we must bear in mind that our consideration does not invoke issues relating to wider 'welfare' issues.

Second, gross output as a measure of production, should be evaluated at **factor cost**, that is excluding taxes on expenditure and including subsidies. Were taxes on expenditure to be included (that is, gross output evaluated at **market prices**) the measurement of production would become dependent upon fiscal policy.

Third, data limitations may seriously hamper the measurement of production as outlined above. For an individual company to measure changes in real production and the input of bought-in goods and services, price and quantity data for bought-in goods and services and goods produced must be available. Government statisticians requiring such data for all sectors of the economy face somewhat greater difficulties (see Appendix I).

The fourth point concerns quality changes. If increased input of capital and/or labour services lead to the same number of goods produced, but these goods are of a higher quality, more work is being done and the measures utilised to represent changes in production should reflect this. Should the improvement in quality stem from more and/or improved bought-in inputs this should be reflected in our indicator of material inputs.

When 'quantity of output of goods' is utilised as an indicator of production, quality changes are not reflected in production changes. Such an indicator requires disaggregation by product categories of different qualities. Thus, the number of passenger cars of different engine capacity levels may be used to represent production for part of the motor vehicle manufacturing industry. In cases where deflated value of output or sales is used the price deflator may be designed to incorporate quality changes, since price data pertaining to technical specifications of the products is usually more readily available.

Quality changes remain a major problem in measuring production, especially where services are produced. There is a practical limit to the extent by which goods can be disaggregated into quality categories and in many cases quality changes do not relate only to a single specified classificatory variable, for example engine capacity, but permuate almost all dimensions of the product. Re-classifying such products into new categories in each period is simply impractical. However, if such quality changes are not reflected in our measure of production, and if the capital and labour services which generate these quality changes are measured properly and incorporated into the estimate of the production function, then the estimate of total factor productivity, and, possibly, the residual of the function will reflect this inability to incorporate such quality changes. Attempts have been made to incorporate quality changes for specific industries by relating the measure of production to intrinsic quality indicators or characteristics of the products concerned, and it is in this direction that the possibility of more correctly incorporating quality changes lies [16].

Hedonic quality functions relate a vector of prices of different varieties of a product, $\underline{P}$, to a matrix $\underline{X}$, whose columns are given by a set of attributes, characteristics specifications derived from consumer surveys or on a priori grounds, and the rows relate to individual varieties of the product (for the respective characteristics). From $\underline{P} = f(\underline{X})$ the implicit 'prices' of each characteristic are estimated by recourse to the coefficients of the regression analysis. Quality is thus summarised by recourse to the component characteristics of a commodity. The meaning of the implicit price of each characteristic has yet to be fully integrated into economic theory, strong links existing with Lancaster's "New Theory of Demand" [17]. At the organisational level in order to fulfil the pragmatic need of adjusting for quality changes, the framework may be useful in cases where the manager can decompose his product into a set of 'characteristics' and believes the consumer reacts (price-wise) to such variations. The relationship between characteristic variations and price variations between varieties of a product may be 'tested' by recourse to the explanatory power of the model [18]. However, our aim is to measure work done or production and an implicit assumption is that the relative price of characteristics of a product estimated from the model $\underline{P} = f(\underline{X})$ equals the marginal product of incorporating the characteristic, these being independent of each other. The addition of a shower and a few trimmings may well turn a 'terraced house' into a 'town house', certainly improving the quality, though contributing to an image which attracts a price over and above that attributable to work done on incorporating the characteristics. Thus, in some contexts hedonic indices may provide a useful framework for adjusting for quality changes, though care should be exercised in order to ensure that the application is appropriate as argued above.

Finally, the problem of incorporating new products should be noted, since changes in physical production cannot be readily measured, there being no prior level of output to compare it with. Incorporating the production of new products into the deflated value of output/sales of other products requires restrictive assumptions as to price changes. A proposed estimate based upon the direct deflation of labour costs and gross profits for the new product is considered in Kmietowicz and Silver [19].

NOTES

1. See Morley, M F, "Value Added: the fashionable choice for annual reports and incentive schemes", The Accountant's Magazine, June 1979, and Appendix II.

2. For details see British Institute of Management, Financial Motivation, An Outline of Some Current Incentive Schemes, Information Note, September 1970, and Silver, M S, "Alternative financial incentive schemes based on value added", Compensation Review: Journal of the American Management Association, Vol.11, 1979, and Appendix II.

3. Wood, E G, "Setting objectives in terms of value added", Long Range Planning, Vol.12, August 1979, and Appendix IV.

4. As noted in Burchell, S, Clubb, C and Hopwood, A, "A message from Mars — and other reminiscences from the past", Accounting, October 1981, see also Appendix IV.

5. Central Statistical Office, National Accounts Statistics Sources and Methods, edited by Rita Maurice, HMSO, London, 1968, p.392.

6. ibid., p.393; also see pp.400–405, and the numerical examples on pp.405 and 406. The actual calculations are more complex than the following discussion indicates, partly because the price adjustment depends to some extent on the number of months purchases in stock.

7. ibid., p.393.

8. Nicholson, J L, "The effects of international trade on the measurement of real national income", The Economic Journal, September 1960, p.609. NB: the words "real national income".

9. See B Hansen, "Double deflation and the value added product: comment", The Review of Economics and Statistics, August 1975; and K Sato, "The Meaning and Measurement of the real value added index", The Review of Economics and Statistics, Vol.58, 1976, pp.434–442.

10. United Nations, Index Numbers of Industrial Production, Studies in Methods, No.1, New York, 1950.

11. M S Silver and P Golder, "Negative value added and the measurement of production changes", Journal of Economic Studies, Vol.8, No.1, 1981.

12. F Divisia, L'indice monetaire et la theorie de la monnaie, Societie Anonyme de Recueil Sirey, Paris, 1926.

13. D W Jorgenson and Z Griliches, "The explanation of productivity change", Review of Economic Studies, Vol.34, 1967, pp.249-283.

14. An alternative index number formula which we also consider to be appropriate is the chained Tornqvist index. this has been used by Tornqvist in the compilation of price indices; see L Tornqvist, "The Bank of Finland's consumption price index", Bank of Finland Monthly Bulletin, 10, 1936, pp.1-18. The formula has also been used by Christensen and Jorgenson; see L R Christensen and D W Jorgenson, "The measurement of US real capital input, 1929-1967", The Review of Income and Wealth, Series 16, 1970, pp.19-50. Details are given in Chapter 3.

15. It is of course possible to conceive of situations in which a fixed base formula would be desirable. For example, if a measure of changes in productivity were used in a company for the purpose of determining bonus payments under an incentive scheme, then the measure of productivity should relate only to the period in question compared with the base period, and not to productivity changes occurring in periods between the current and base period as is the case with the chained index; on this point see M S Silver, "Alternative financial incentive schemes based on value added", Journal of the American Management Association, Compensation Review, Third quarter, 1979. However, when in macro-economic analysis a dynamic as opposed to comparative static measure of change is required, the chained index is considered to be more appropriate. The use of the Divisia index - and therefore of the chained index as its discrete approximation - has also been justified by economic theory (see Sato, 1976, op.cit.). Furthermore, the Divisia index also performs well with respect to Fisher's mathematical tests for index numbers; see I Fisher, The Making of Index Numbers, Houghton Mifflin, Boston, 1922. These and further index number issues will be discussed in the next chapter.

16. See Griliches, Z (ed.), <u>Price Indexes and Quality Change: Studies in New Methods of Measurement</u>, Harvard University Press, Cambridge, 1971; Cowling, K and Cubbin, J, "Hedonic price indexes for UK cars", <u>Economic Journal</u>, 82, 1972, pp.963–978.

17. Lancaster, K, "A new approach to consumer theory", <u>Journal of Political Economy</u>, 74, 1966, pp.132–157 and Lancaster, K, <u>Consumer Demand: A New Approach</u>, Columbia Studies in Economics, No.5, Columbia University Press, New York and London, 1971.

18. For an interesting discussion of the relationship between economic theory and Hedonic indices, and the meaning of the latter see Triplett, J, "Consumer Demand and Characteristics of Consumption Goods", in N E Terleckyj (ed.), <u>Household Production and Consumption</u>, Conference on Research in Income and Wealth, <u>Studies in Income and Wealth</u>, 40, NBER, New York, 1975, pp.305–325, and Ohta, M and Griliches, Z, "Automobile Prices Revisited: Extensions of the Hedonic Hypothesis", in N E Terleckyj (ed.) ibid., pp.325–391.

19. See Kmietowicz, Z W and Silver, M S, "New products (industries) and the index of industrial production", <u>Journal of Development Studies</u>, 16, 4, 1980.

3 Some further index number issues

The concern of this chapter is with the choice of index number formula for the removal of price changes from changes in money values in order to monitor changes in physical outputs and inputs. The discussion will be outlined in terms of the measurement of gross output in physical terms, though the principles apply to factor and material inputs and net output.

The need to discuss the question of choice between alternative index number formulae arises from first, the wide range of formulae available. Irving Fisher in his classic work in 1922 listed 126 index number formulae [1]. Second, criteria by which index number formulae are deemed to be appropriate are by no means accepted. Forsyth and Fowler [2], in considering an appropriate formula for a Consumer Price Index, believed representativity to be the central criterion, whilst Fisher argued that an 'ideal' index should be one which satisfied a number of (albeit inconsistent, see Eichhorn [3]) mathematical tests he proposed. Much attention has focussed on the derivation of index numbers from economic theory [4]. Theil derived his 'appropriate' formula from a 'statistical' approach [5] – though this has been given some meaning in economic theory – and Stuvel and Banerjee [6] from a factorial approach. Third, alternative formulae may yield quite different results. For example, Table 3.1 shows fictitious data for two periods as calculated by the Laspeyres and

Paasche formulae, the Laspeyres showing an increase in real output of 16 per cent, whilst the Paasche yields an increase of 41.67 per cent.

Table 3.1
Difference between Laspeyres and Paasche

	Year 0			Year 1		
	Price	Quantity	Value	Price	Quantity	Value
Product A	6	500	3,000	12	800	9,600
Product B	10	200	2,000	6	100	600
			5,000			10,200

Laspeyres: Year 0 = 100.0; Year 1 = 116.0
Paasche : Year 0 = 100.0; Year 1 = 141.67

The ratio of Paasche (P) to Laspeyres (L) is given by:

$$\frac{P}{L} = 1 \stackrel{-}{+} r \frac{\sigma_p}{L_p} \frac{\sigma_q}{L_q}$$

where

r is the weighted correlation coefficient between price and quantity relatives;

σ_p and σ_q are weighted standard deviations of price and quantity relatives respectively;

L_p and L_q are the (weighted mean) Laspeyres indices of price and quantity relatives respectively.

For the difference between chained Laspeyres (Paasche) and fixed base Laspeyres (Paasche) see Forsyth and Fowler [2].

Laspeyres, Paasche and Fisher's 'ideal' index

The Laspeyres and Paasche quantity indices are repeated below by eqns (1) and (2), respectively, for a comparison between a base period and a current period (denoted by subscripts b and c, respectively; P and Q denote price and quantity of outputs and the summation extends over items produced:

$$\text{Laspeyres:} \quad \frac{\Sigma \ P_b Q_c}{\Sigma \ P_b Q_b} = \frac{\Sigma \ P_b Q_b (Q_c/Q_b)}{\Sigma \ P_b Q_b} \qquad \ldots (1)$$

$$\text{Paasche:} \quad \frac{\Sigma \ P_c Q_c}{\Sigma \ P_c Q_b} = \frac{\Sigma \ P_c Q_c}{\Sigma \ P_c Q_c (Q_b/Q_c)} \qquad \ldots (2)$$

The relative importance or weight given to production changes between products is that pertaining to the base period for the Laspeyres index and the current period for the Paasche index. Adopting a criterion of purpose, the Laspeyres answers the question: what is the change in output in the current period compared with the base period measured at base period prices (or utilising the mix or relative importance of products in the base period)? Similarly, the Paasche provides such a comparison on the basis of the price mix or weights of the current period remaining constant. If these comparisons are meaningful to an organisation the relevant formulae are appropriate. However, questions are rarely phrased so succinctly, and neither are particularly meaningful. Economic theory has shown the Laspeyres formula to suffer from a substitution bias. For a consumer price index, assuming indifference curves are concave to the origin (that is, a negative price—quantity relationship) the Laspeyres index will overstate a 'true' cost—of—living index. The Laspeyres price index, in keeping the same basket or mix of goods in the base period, does not take into account the increase in satisfaction or utility stemming from consumers substituting cheaper goods for more expensive goods, that is, changing the mix of the basket, as relative prices change [7]. Konus, Wald and Schultz [8] demonstrated that a 'true'index defined from economic theory should lie between (or be equal to) Laspeyres and Paasche. However, Samuelson and Swamy [9] have emphasised the point that these formulae only act as limits to the 'true' index as defined from economic theory if the underlying utility (for consumer prices) or production (for output and inputs) functions are homothetic. In the non—homothetic case the Laspeyres acts as an upper bound, there being no double bounds.

Whilst much of this work was developed for price indices, the analysis can be applied to production indices. Laspeyres and Paasche provide the limits to the 'true' index if the production function is homothetic. However, in this instance the Laspeyres is the lower limit and Paasche the upper limit (see Sato [10]). This reversal of positions stems from the concave to the origin assumption behind production possibility frontiers (as opposed to convex indifference curves) whereby production is substituted towards goods with relatively large increases (as in the example in Table 3.1). Thus the above discussion provides a basis whereupon the bias in alternative formulae may be derived.

At first sight, economic theory provides some justification for the adoption of Fisher's 'ideal' index. This index is a geometric average of Laspeyres and Paasche and therefore must lie between the two. Fisher's 'ideal' index, given by:

$$\sqrt{\left[\frac{\Sigma \; P_b Q_c}{\Sigma \; P_b Q_b} \; x \; \frac{\Sigma \; P_c Q_c}{\Sigma \; P_c Q_b} \right]} \qquad \qquad \ldots (3)$$

was called 'ideal' owing to its property of satisfying a number (though not all) of a series of mathematical tests. Whilst such tests were not consistent (that is, no formula could satisfy all of the tests as demonstrated by Eichhorn [11]) these tests are useful for evaluating properties of alternative formulae, but purpose and meaning remain primary considerations [12]. Furthermore, whilst the true index may lie between, or be equal to Fisher's 'ideal' index, this is but one point in the Paasche–Laspeyres interval (including, in the case of no substitution, Laspeyres or Paasche themselves). As such, we must be careful not to provide too much justification to Fisher's 'ideal' index on these grounds. Samuelson and Swamy [13] have shown Fisher's 'ideal' index to be a second–order approximation to a 'true' homothetic index, though if the underlying function is not homothetic the index may yield quite inaccurate results. Homotheticity is not as unrealistic an assumption in production function work (satisfied by, for example, the Cobb–Douglas function) as for utility functions for consumer price indexes. The choice of appropriate formulae can be seen to benefit from an a priori notion of the form of the underlying function. In particular, Fisher's 'ideal' index can be shown to be 'exact' (as opposed to a second–order approximation) if the function is of a quadratic homothetic form.

The chain method

An alternative approach to dealing with the inability of the Laspeyres index to cater for substitution of products is to regularly change or shift the base of the index. The chain method, as noted in Chapter 2, for a comparison between, say,

1975 and 1983, would compute annual indices or 'links' for 1976 compared with 1975; 1977 with 1976; 1978 with 1977, etc., and make the final comparison between 1983 and 1975 by combining the annual link changes through successive multiplication. Thus where $I_{76,75}$ is the index comparing 1976 with 1975, the chain index for a comparison between 1983 and 1975 is given by:

$$Ci_{83,75} = I_{76,75} \times I_{77,76} \times I_{78,77} \times I_{79,78} \times I_{80,79} \times I_{81,80}$$

$$\times I_{82,81} \times I_{83,82} \qquad \ldots (4)$$

The choice of which formula to use for the calculation of each link is of importance only if the time interval for each link is relatively large, in the sense that it incorporates changes in the output mix of products produced. If the Laspeyres is used it would incorporate a substitution bias for output changes occurring within the link interval. However, the continual, say, annual changes in weights may offset much of the bias stemming from utilising a fixed-base Laspeyres formula. For a production index the ability of the chain method to account for substitution should allow for the chained Laspeyres and Paasche indices to lie between fixed-base Laspeyres and Paasche indices and empirical results (albeit in terms of consumption and price indices for which the relative positions of Laspeyres and Paasche are reversed) lend some support to this [14].

The chain index has received much support as the natural discrete approximation to the Divisia integral (index). This integral, developed by Divisia [15] has been adopted to form the basis of a system of accounting for growth [16].

The total output, in our case by an organisation, given by PQ, is equal to the inputs to the organisation, given by $\Sigma p_i q_i$, that is:

$$PQ = \Sigma \ p_i q_i \qquad \ldots (5)$$

Assuming all variables are continuous functions of time, the total differential of eqn (5) is

$$PdQ + QdP = \Sigma \ p_i dq_i + \Sigma \ q_i dp_i \qquad \ldots (6)$$

Dividing eqn (6) by eqn (5)

$$\frac{dQ}{Q} + \frac{dP}{P} = \frac{\Sigma \ p_i dq_i}{\Sigma \ p_i q_i} + \frac{\Sigma \ q_i dp_i}{\Sigma \ p_i q_i}$$

$$= \frac{\Sigma \ p_i q_i (dq_i/q_i)}{\Sigma \ p_i q_i} + \frac{\Sigma \ p_i q_i (dp_i/p_i}{\Sigma \ p_i q_i}$$

$$= \Sigma \ w_i \frac{dq_i}{q_i} + \Sigma \ w_i \frac{dp_i}{p_i} \qquad \ldots \ (7)$$

where

$$w_i = \frac{p_i q_i}{\Sigma \ p_i q_i}$$

From eqn (7) it is natural to equate the component parts of the equation, that is:

$$\frac{dP}{P} = \Sigma \ w_i \frac{dp_i}{p_i} \qquad \ldots \ (8)$$

$$\frac{dQ}{Q} = \Sigma \ w_i \frac{dq_i}{q_i} \qquad \ldots \ (9)$$

Considering the physical output component, eqn (9),

$$\frac{dQ}{Q} = \Sigma \ w_i \frac{dq_i}{q_i} \qquad \ldots \ (10)$$

and

$$d(\ln Q) = \Sigma \ w_i d(\ln \ q_i) \qquad \ldots \ (11)$$

To find the value of the quantity index from origin, 0, to a future period, t, the differential quantity index has to be integrated over all values of p and q in the interval. Let

$$\Sigma \ w_i d(\ln \ q_i) = f(t)dt \qquad \ldots \ (12)$$

and

$$d(\ln Q) = f(t)dt \qquad \ldots \ (13)$$

which on integration equals

$$\ln Q_t - \ln Q_0 = \int_0^t f(s)ds = F(t) \qquad \dots (14)$$

and the value of the index in period t is given by:

$$Q_t = Q_0 \exp \int_0^t f(s)ds = Q_0 \exp[F(t)] \qquad \dots (15)$$

Now this definition of the index can be applied to decompose a value change into the price and quantity components ($PQ=\Sigma pq$) or as the only framework by which variations in the value of a plant's output is accurately and totally made up from variations in the price and quantity components of inputs to the plant as long homotheticity prevails [17]. As such, the above derivation provides strong support for the use of eqn (15) as an appropriate index number for productivity measurement. There is, of course, a complication. The Divisia integral is a theoretical construct. As output changes through infinitesimal points in time the weights of the index are automatically adjusted to ensure they reflect the plant's product mix. The curvilinear integral index requires price and quantity data for each infinitesimal point in time.

It should be apparent from the above discussion that the chain base index provides a natural, discrete approximation to the continuous Divisia index. The chain index regularly adjusts its weights over time, thus being an appropriate discrete approximation to the Divisia index, which continually adjusts its weights over infinitesimal points of continuous time. Two (related) problems should be noted. The first concerns the choice of formula for the links of the index. As the time interval of the links become smaller, the choice of formula becomes of less importance since at the limit (infinitesimal time intervals) all formulae yield the same result, the Divisia index. However, as will be noted later, economic theory can provide us with some indication as to the choice of link formula. The second problem is that the chain index may drift under conditions of quantity oscillations. Forsyth and Fowler [18] have discussed this problem at length, a possible solution being the choice of link formula.

Purpose

The chain index has received some theoretical justification as the natural approximation to the Divisia index. This provides a system of productivity indices derived from a framework which, assuming homotheticity, allows the contribution of each input to be appropriately measured, and be combined to fully account for output changes. The use of alternative index number formulae would not provide for a system of productivity measures which fully account for growth [19].

However, such a system is but one purpose of productivity measures, and purpose, that is, the criterion of answering meaningful, valid or useful questions, must remain central to the discussion. Consider an organisation for which the level of services provided by capital has remained constant over time, and no economies of scale, stemming for reorganisation of the work process, etc., have taken place. Trends in labour productivity may be evaluated in terms of, say, real net output per (homogenous) man-hour.

The index number formula utilised to (double) deflate net output over a period of, say, five years, may be the chain index. A characteristic of the chain (and Divisia) index is its path dependence (except under certain conditions [20]). Since the index is evaluated for a series of discrete intervals over the five-year period its value may depend not only on the level of output in the first and last period, but in all discrete periods evaluated within the interval. Chain (Divisia) indices for two different plants may yield different results for a comparison between period 0 and period 5, not because output levels differ in these two periods but because the production paths or output levels and mixes the plants have followed between the initial and final period have differed. Whether such an index is appropriate depends on the purpose of the index. If it is to monitor changes in labour productivity, in a dynamic sense, over the interval it is appropriate since the production process has 'lived' through the output path and output mixes. The relevance of the index can be best illustrated by reference to the consumer price index. Since consumers purchase the goods over the interval and enjoy the fruits of changes in relative prices by altering their consumption mix over the period, there is a distinct advantage in an index which follows the path of price changes updating the weights (consumption patterns) regularly.

However, consider the case of a financial incentive scheme linked to labour productivity trends (a mechanism existing to take account of changes in the ratio of capital to labour). Employees and management, having agreed upon a base level of labour productivity, may wish the bonuses to be affected by a comparison between labour productivity in the current and base periods only. If labour productivity is high in period 5, but had been low in periods 1, 2, 3 and 4, a 'desirable' scheme may wish the comparison (and bonus) for period 5 to relate only to productivity in that period compared with the initial base period. The chain index would incorporate the effects of production in the intervening period. As such, a fixed base index which makes a direct binary comparison between the base and current period may be appropriate (for example, Laspeyres, Paasche or Fisher's 'ideal'). Such indices answer questions pertaining more to comparative static analysis than the dynamic analysis of the chain index. In the latter case the superior representativity of the chain index, in that it adjusts for changes in the relative importance of outputs (or inputs), facilitates the introduction of new products [21], can deal more readily with quality changes [22], can help in problems arising from negative weights [23] and its justification as an approximation to the Divisia integral argues well for its adoption.

Economic theory

Recent work in this area has provided some guidelines as to the choice of appropriate formulae. Particular index number formulae have been shown to be 'exact' or correspond to 'true' indices derived from production functions of particular forms. Given some indication as to the form of the underlying production function, an appropriate formulae can be utilised. The Laspeyres formula has been found to correspond to a function with fixed coefficients, thus allowing no substitution between commodities. Diewert and Lau [24] have demonstrated that within the class of once differentiable functions the Tornqvist formula [25] given by Q_c/Q_b where

$$\ln(Q_c/Q_b) = \sum \bar{w}_{it} (\ln q_{i,c} - \ln q_{i,b}) \qquad \ldots (16)$$

and

$$\bar{w}_{it} = 0.5(w_{i,c} + w_{i,b})$$

is exact if and only if the function is a member of the class of homogeneous of degree one transcendental logarithmic functions. Christensen and Manser [26] have taken this result out of the realms of theory and, for US data pertaining to meat and garden produce, estimated Consumer Price Indices utilising a transcendental logarithmic form (which possesses a number of attractive properties including the ability to test for some of the underlying assumptions built into economic theory of this kind, in this case additivity and homotheticity). They compared the results from conventional index number formulae to those estimated from economic theory (via indirect utility functions), paying particular attention to the Tornqvist chained index. Needless to say, the Tornqvist chained index provided results similar to those estimated from a homothetic transcendental logarithmic utility function.

Thus our problem of appropriate formula can be identified more in terms of what is appropriate to meet the corresponding underlying function. The list of functions and appropriate formulae may be expanded to include Fisher's 'ideal' index is exact if and only if the function is the square root of a homogeneous of degree one (homothetic) quadratic function; within the class of once continuous differentiable two factor productions the Sato-Vartia index [27] is exact if and only if the function is a member of the class of homogeneous of degree one constant-elasticity-of-substitution (CES) functions and the weighted geometric mean of output changes is exact for a Cobb-Douglas production function. For further details the reader is referred to Diewert and Lau [28].

The point to be made is that the 'appropriate' formula may be conceived in terms of: appropriate for particular functions to be indexed. Given some a priori notion as to the form of the underlying function, a suitable choice may be made. Such results correspond to an alternative formulation by means of numerical analysis [29]. However, the degree of sophistication for the analysis referred to in this section argues against it in practice. In theory it provides a basis for choosing between alternative formula. Given a practitioner with sufficient experience of the mathematical forms an attempt to translate each form into the realism of the characteristics of a production process to make an a priori judgement as to which function is likely to represent the process, and thus the appropriate index number formula, requires some expertise, though it is not beyond the realms of possibility. Estimation of the underlying functions and testing their nature through economic misspecification analysis is likely to be further away.

Yet this chapter, in not being able to (nor wishing to) ignore the valid contribution from economic theory believes a wider awareness of the principles of choosing appropriate formula may stem from a consideration of the purpose of the measures. In particular, a move away from the traditional fixed-base Laspeyres and Paasche formulae and development of the rationale for a chain index may serve a useful function. As the time interval for each link becomes smaller, the difference between utilising different formulae becomes smaller. As 'compromise solutions' a chained Fisher's 'ideal' index or Tornqvist index have been found in both theory and practice to be 'safe' approximations [30]. Diewert [31] defined a number of index number formulae to be **superlative** in that they, aside from being exact for particular functional forms, provided a second-order approximation to any underlying homogeneous of degree one function. The Tornqvist and Fisher's 'ideal' index were both found to be superlative. When price and quantity changes are small superlative indices give 'virtually the same answer even if economic agents are not engaged in optimising behaviour' [33]. Thus the Tornqvist and Fisher's 'ideal' index may be preferred to Laspeyres and Paasche since the latter correspond to a restrictive fixed coefficient function (allowing for no substitution) whilst the former are exact for more flexible functional forms and provide second-order approximations to other homogeneous forms. As a formula for chaining, or using for comparative static analysis, superlative indices have much to commend them.

Furthermore, superlative indices have been shown by Diewert [33] to be approximately consistent in aggregation in that the results from two-stage aggregation will be approximately equal to single-stage aggregation. In practical index number work groups of products may be compiled in two stages. Superlative index numbers compiled in two stages yield approximately the same result as if compiled in one stage, that is, they possess consistency-in-aggregation. It may be argued that Laspeyres and Paasche possess perfect consistency-in-aggregation. However, these formulae correspond to restrictive forms of underlying functions.

Whilst some support is derived from economic theory for superlative index numbers if the form of the production function is not known, and for corresponding exact index numbers if some indication of the functional form is available, the use of chaining has not been referred to. Superlative and exact index numbers are suitable for individual links of the chain. The economic theory of index numbers is derived from considering binary comparisons. However, an implicit assumption of the theory is that the prevailing technology embodied in the functional form of the production function does not change. Chaining provides an opportunity to provide some allowance for changes in the technological relationship implicit in the form of the production function either by utilising the same form (formula) with different parameters, or changing the form (formula) of the function.

In demonstrating the assumptions behind alternative formulae in terms of the nature of underlying functions, more complex notions are being introduced. Whilst purpose, as a criterion, may override guidelines provided by economic theory, it is with economic theory that the assumptions behind the use of alternative formulae may be derived. Ignoring the contribution from economic theory does not, to quote Samuelson and Swamy's concluding warnings [34], make the use of 'naive measurements that untutored commonsense always longs for' any more valid: 'We must accept the sad facts of life, and be grateful for the more complicated procedures economic theory devises.'

Thus in (the more common) areas where a notion as to the form of the underlying production function cannot be discerned superlative index numbers are advocated. The process of chaining is also to be applied for reasons outlined. Recommended formulae include the chained Tornqvist index and the chained Fisher's 'ideal' index. The former was used to calculate real production and real input changes and to combine changes in aggregate inputs into a measure of changes in total input (productivity) in the illustration in Chapter 1.

NOTES

1. Fisher, I, <u>The Making of Index Numbers</u>, Houghton Mifflin, Boston, 1922.

2. Forsyth, F G and Fowler, R F, 'The theory and practice of chain price index numbers', <u>Journal of the Royal Statistical Society</u>, A, 144, 2, pp.224–247, 1981.

3. Eichhorn, W, 'Fisher's tests revisited', <u>Econometrica</u>, 44, 2, 1976.

4. See Frisch, R, 'Annual survey of general economic theory: the problem of index numbers', <u>Econometrica</u>, 4, 7, 1936, and Afriat, S N, <u>The Price Index</u>, University Press, Cambridge, 1977, for a survey.

5. Theil, H, <u>Economic and Information Theory</u>, North-Holland, Amsterdam, 1967.

6. Stuvel, G, 'A new index number formula', <u>Econometrica</u>, 25, 1, pp.123–131, 1957, and Banerjee, K S, <u>Cost of Living Index Numbers: Practice, Precision and Theory</u>, Marcel Dekker Inc, New York, 1975.

7. Braithwait, S D, 'The substitution bias of the Laspeyres price index: an analysis using estimated cost-of-living indexes', <u>The American Economic Review</u>, 70, 1, pp.64–77, 1980.

8. Konus, A A, 'The problem of the true index of the cost of living', <u>Econometrica</u>, 7, pp.10–24, 1939; Wald, A, 'A new formula for the index of cost of living', <u>Econometrica</u>, 7, pp.319–331, 1939; and Schultz, H, 'A misunderstanding in index number theory: the true Konus condition on cost of living index numbers and its limitations', <u>Econometrica</u>, 7, pp.1–9, 1939.

9. Samuelson, P A and Swamy, S, 'Invariant economic index numbers and canonical duality: survey and synthesis', <u>American Economic Review</u>, 64, pp.566–593, 1974.

10. Sato, K, 'The meaning and measurement of the real value added index', <u>Review of Economics and Statistics</u>, 58, pp.434–442, 1976.

11. Eichhorn, op. cit., 1976.

12. See also, on this issue, Winkler, W, 'Older and newer ways of solving index number problems', Bulletin de L'Institut de Statistique, 34.2, 1954.

13. Samuelson and Swamy, op.cit., 1974.

14. Fowler, R F, 'Some problems of index number construction', Studies in Official Statistics, Research Series, No.3, H.M.S.O., London, 1970.

15. Divisia, F, 'L'indice monetaire et la theorie de la monnaie', Revue Economique Politique, Societe Anonyme de Recueil Sirey, Paris, 1925.

16. See Jorgenson and Griliches, op.cit., 1967.

17. Jorgenson, D W and Griliches, Z, 'Divisia index numbers and productivity measurement', The Review of Income and Wealth', 17, pp.227–229, 1971; Hulten, C R, 'Divisia index numbers', Econometrica, 41, pp.1017–1026, 1973; and Diewert, W E, 'Aggregation problems in the measurement of capital' in Dan Usher (ed.), The Measurement of Capital, National Bureau of Economic Research, 1980, Studies in Income and Wealth, Vol.45, N.B.E.R, Chicago and London.

18. Forsyth and Fowler, op.cit. 1981.

19. See Jorgenson and Griliches, op.cit., 1967 and 1971); Samuelson and Swamy, op.cit., 1974; Sato, op.cit., 1976; Hulten, op.cit., 1973; and Diewert, op.cit., 1980.

20. See Hulten, op.cit., 1973.

21. Kmietowicz, Z W and Silver, M S, 'New products and the index of industrial production', Journal of Development Studies, 16, 4, pp.463–467, 1980.

22. Kmietowicz, Z W and Rwamasaka, H M K, 'An index of industrial production for Uganda, 1963–1971', East African Economic Review, 8, 2, 1976.

23. Silver, M S and Golder, P, 'Negative value added and the measurement of production changes', Journal of Economic Studies, 8, 1, 1981.

24. Diewert, W E, 'Exact and superlative index numbers', Journal of Econometrics, 4, 115-145, 1976; and Lau, L, 'On exact index numbers', The Review of Economics and Statistics', 61, pp.73-82, 1979.

25. Tornqvist, L, 'The Bank of Finland's consumption price index', Bank of Finland Monthly Bulletin, 10, pp.1-8, 1936.

26. Christensen, L R and Manser, M E, 'Cost-of-living indexes and price indexes for US meat and produce, 1947-1971', in N E Terleckyj (ed.), Household Production and Consumption, Studies in Income and Wealth, Vol.40, National Bureau of Economic Research, New York, 1975.

27. Sato, K, 'Generalised ideal cost-of-living indexes and indirect utility functions', State University of New York at Buffalo Economics Discussion Paper, 290, 1973; and Sato, K, 'The ideal log-change index number, Review of Economics and Statistics, 58, pp.223-238, 1976.

28. Diewert, W E, op.cit, 1976, and Lau, op.cit, 1979.

29. See Trivedi, P K, 'Some discrete approximations to Divisia integral indices', International Economic Review, 22, 1, pp.71-77, 1981.

30. See Theil, op.cit, 1967; Diewert, op.cit, 1976; Tornqvist, op.cit, 1936; and Samuelson and Swamy, op.cit, 1974.

31. Diewert, op.cit, 1976; Diewert, W E, 'Superlative index numbers and consistency of aggregation', Econometrica, 46, 4, 1978, and Diewert, op.cit, 1980.

32. Diewert, op.cit, p.452, 1980.

33, Diewert, op.cit, 1978 and 1980.

34. Samuelson and Swamy, op.cit, 1974.

4 The input of labour

Labour input and the flow of man-hours worked

Labour productivity may be measured by gross output per unit of labour input. Changes in labour productivity may be measured by changes in "real" gross output relative to changes in labour inputs [1]. What is the best way to measure the input of labour?

The labour inputs to an enterprise may, in the first instance, be measured in terms of the number of persons working in the enterprise. Here we encounter a problem. Gross output relates to a flow during a period, generally such as a year. Yet the number of persons working at any one time during the year may vary. Therefore, the number of persons working at, say, the end of a period may be an unsatisfactory indicator of the number of persons working in that enterprise over the course of the whole year.

It is therefore desirable to measure the number of persons working at two or more equally-spaced moments during the year. The average of these equally-spaced numbers then more accurately represents the number working during the course of the whole year. The count of workers may be done twice yearly, quarterly or monthly. Clearly, the more frequent the count, the more accurate and appropriate is the resulting average for purposes of calculating productivity.

However, the average number of persons working during the year may still be an unsatisfactory measure of the actual flow of input of labour services during the course of the year, particularly when it comes to making comparisons among enterprises or industries, or over a period of years. This is because the number of hours worked during the year may differ or may change. For example, two enterprises may have the same average number of workers, yet one enterprise may get more input from its workers if they work more hours per week.

It is therefore desirable to measure the labour input with regard to the number of man-hours worked during the period under consideration. This converts the measurement of labour input from a stock of workers to a flow of worker-hours per period, and this latter flow is more accurately related to the flow of resulting real gross output produced by that labour time.

The importance of distinguishing between the number of employees and man-hours worked has been highlighted by Craine [2]. The Cobb-Douglas production function is modified to allow an index of hours worked per period, H, to enter the function independently of the number of employees, thus not constraining the elasticity of output with respect to number of employees, to be the same as that with respect to hours worked. Thus:

$$O = Ae^{pt}L^{\alpha}K^{\beta}H^{\gamma} \qquad \qquad \ldots (1)$$

where Ae^{pt} represents technical progress not 'embodied' in capital, assumed to follow an exponential time trend, L the number of employees, K the input of capital services, and H the index of number of hours worked.

We have noted that the average production of employees may be an inadequate measure of labour productivity, since it does not take account of variations in the number of hours worked per employee and empirical work based on expression (1) has shown the output elasticities of number of workers, α, and hours worked, γ, to differ [3]. Thus, if 'number of workers' is used as an indicator for labour input in any comparison of labour productivity either between establishments or sectors, or over time for a particular establishment or sector, man-hours worked provides a more appropriate indicator since the man-hours worked per employee may well differ between establishments or over time. Yet the input of labour services may vary within or between particular man-hours worked. Is it necessary to adjust for such changes?

If our purpose is to reflect such changes in the measure of labour productivity the answer is no. For example, the very purpose of the measure may be to (partly) reflect the fact that the input of labour services has been greater in one period than another for which the input of labour services was, say, haphazard. In both periods man-hours worked may be identical, but in one period labour input per man-hour may be higher thus leading to a higher level of real production. The measurement of labour productivity based on man-hours worked will reflect this difference and this may be the purpose of the measure.

However, if our purpose is to account for or 'explain' variations in output, identifying the relative contributions of labour and capital input, then our aim is to measure the changes in the input of labour services and relate such changes to production changes. Labour productivity can be calculated by recourse to a number of indicators, the differences between the ensuing series reflecting that element due to variations in hours worked or effort within or between hours worked.

Denison [4] has argued in favour of the use of number of employees as opposed to man-hours worked as an indicator of labour input. He argues that as hours are lengthened increased fatigue is accompanied by deterioration in the quantity and quality of output, absenteeism, late arrival and early leaving to conduct personal affairs. Similarly, shortening of hours is argued to lead to increased output owing to less fatigue etc., and a tightening up of operations (though the latter should not be designated as labour input). However, utilising (on the above grounds) 'number of employees' as opposed to 'man-hours worked' to measure the flow of labour services requires that the output per worker remains the same in spite of hours worked. Whilst it is correct to acknowledge that output per man-hour may vary and the direction is likely to result in a negative correlation between hours worked and output per man-hour, this is not to argue for the use of number of employees as an indicator of labour input. Even if changes in hours worked are offset by changes in output per man-hour, in order to explain, and provide a rational basis for planning, the inputs to the production process the separate specification of these influences is required. Information to the effect that an x

per cent increase in hours worked for a 'type' of labour will
lead to a y per cent decrease in output for these additional
hours worked provides a role in any decision to increase
labour services using the existing stock of labour, as well as
explaining a contribution to production changes. A diagram
relating total output and length of the work week for periods
when other factors (for example, capital/labour substitution)
have remained constant or can be adjusted for, should provide
a useful mechanism for this purpose.

The heterogeneity of labour

So far the discussion has implicitly assumed labour input to
be homogenous. However, our stock of labour may not be
homogenous performing different work and possessing different
skills. The aggregation of different types of labour, say in
terms of number of employees and/or man–hours worked,
requires the marginal rate of substitution between any two
'types' of labour to be independent of capital. To take
account of variations over time in the relative composition
of different types or categories of labour, changes in the
input of labour services may be measured as an index of the
weighted average (using the Tornqvist formula – Chapter 3) of
the rates of growth of different categories of labour. The
weights used are based on the relative share in labour
compensation of different types of labour [5]. We are thus
using the relative prices of labour as an indicator of the
relative services provided by different types of labour,
which may not always be valid. Further disaggregation may
allow for the identification of weighted inputs of labour,
not only by 'type' of work, but sex, years of experience,
years of completed education, attendance or otherwise of
particular training courses and so forth, should detailed
information be available. Gollop and Jorgenson, in a study of
the United States, broke labour input down into 81,600 cells
classified by 51 industries, 2 sexes, 2 employment classes, 8
age groups, 10 occupational groups and 5 education groups
[6]. Relative prices of labour may not reflect the relative
contribution of categories of labour to production. However,
the continual up–dating of the weights in a Divisia (chained)
index will at least attempt to ensure that changes in the
relative importance of different categories of labour (albeit
reflected by the relative prices) are accounted for [7] and,
given no notion as to the form of the underlying function, a
superlative index will curtail errors arising from
inappropriate index number formulae.

It has been noted that account needs to be taken of the cumulative experience or 'learning process' of labour, changes in the extent and nature of on and off-the-job training, variations in the level and nature of pre-employment education. If we conceive of education as an investment in human capital, the flow of labour services per stock of labour may change owing to educational deepening, as a given level of education of the workforce is increased, or educational widening, as a given level of education is distributed over a wider sector of the workforce [8]. Needless to say, the extent to which an improved pre-employment education will contribute to a growth in output will vary between types of work and the extent to which the age structure of workforce becomes younger. Yet such skills may also contribute to growth if they lead to a closer identification of workers with company aims, facilitate the acceptance and understanding of new, improved modes of production or provoke innovation and reduced quit rates [9]. Furthermore, education may increase the skills and versatility of labour, thus allowing transfers of resources to 'newer' more 'productive' areas. The individual's awareness of job opportunities may also be heightened, thus increasing the possibility of being employed where his marginal product is greatest [11].

Oatey [10] distinguished between:

(1) training – as an activity which deliberately attempts to improve a person's skill at a task; and

(2) learning from experience – as an improvement of a person's skill by the normal execution of a task, and with no deliberate attempt at improvement.

We formalise this taxonomy in Diagram 4.1. Note that "intervention" denotes any deliberate attempt to change the 'normal' working practice for the purpose of skill acquisition. The methods are not indivisible; for example, formal training may be combined with irregular (eg. occasionally supervised) on-the-job training and an overall strategy may encompass a sequence of methods. We can conceptualise some substitution between methods for a particular technology for intervals in time with an optimum strategy being derived which takes into account the cost of alternative training schemes (including the opportunity cost of supervision) and expected marginal productivities of trainees arising from different schemes.

Diagram 4.1
Taxonomy of Skill Acquisition

	Continuous supervision/ training	Irregular supervision/ training	No supervision/ intervention
On-the-job	Continuous on-the-job training	Irregular on-the-job training	Learning from experience
Off-the-job	Formal training	Informal training	Being idle

Increases in the flow of labour services due to training or education may be difficult to distinguish. In some instances the output of employees before and after undertaking a training period may be monitored as long as technology and work organisation remains constant or data can be adjusted for the effects of such factors. Such monitoring would have to be long-term given the possibility of a short-term increase in output arising from an initial interest in the work (or rest from work) stemming from training only to fall-off in the long-run. However, in many circumstances such data may not be available and the classification of employees into different skill groups is only possible. Increases in employees in 'more skilled' groups and corresponding decreases in 'less skilled' groups may ensue from training (though differential rates of leavers (voluntary and otherwise) also imposes on the aggregate skill-mix). The combination of increases and decreases for such groups would take place via the Tornqvist formula proposed in Chapter 3, their relative importance being designated by the price mechanism. It is, therefore, of interest to consider again the rationale behind the use of relative prices for skills of labour as an indicator of relative 'importance' or contribution to the production process of different groupings of labour.

Marginal productivity theory suggests, under conditions of perfect competition, that the marginal product of a 'type' of labour will be equated with its price or wage rate [12]. Since the benefits of training are not confined to a 'one-off' increase in production, there is a need to sum the discounted benefits or products expected over future time periods. Thus training should only be undertaken (for cost minimisation purposes) if the discounted benefits accruing to the organisation from the training cover costs and compare well with alternative projects, bearing in mind the 'risk' element in alternative projects. In the case of training the risk element includes the employee being trained not absorbing the required skills (for whatever reason) and utilising them effectively and the probability of employees leaving the organisation during a period when the additional production stemming from training may be utilised. Becker [12] believed the quit rate will be lower if skills are made to be more specific, though rigidities in the labour market may curtail the strength of any relationship between the generality of training and quit rate [13].

Under the following conditions training may be incurred:

$$MP_0 + \sum_{t=1}^{n} \frac{MP_t}{(1+r)^t} \geqslant w_0 + K_0 + \sum_{t=1}^{n} \frac{w_t}{(1+r)^t}$$

where   r is the discount rate;
         n the number of periods of employment;
         K_0 is training expenditure assumed to be once and for all in period 0;
         MP_t and w_t the marginal product and wage rate in period t.

Adopting this framework some market rigidities are required for the organisation in subsequent periods has to pay a wage rate possibly less than the marginal product in order to recoup initial training costs. However, under perfect competition a competitor may offer a higher wage rate equal to the trained employee's marginal product having not to cover training costs. Thus, even within the restrictive marginal productivity framework problems arise. Add to these the real rigidities of the labour market, part of which includes varying degrees of monopsonist power between employees, and relative prices may not be confidently utilised to reflect the relative contribution to production of employees. Attempts to explain variations in wage rates for an individual over his life by recourse to schooling and training as investments in human capital augmenting the productive powers of labour have had little success [14]. Though this is not to say that at the organisational level the measurement problems will be intractable, since output patterns per employee over time (experience) or between training phases may be discerned whilst account is taken of other variables.

Given that relative prices provide the only practical and meaningful variable for a weighting system, adjustments for 'obvious' discrepancies can be made. For example, if trained employees and untrained employees are paid at the same rate the 'price' of trained employees may be marked up by the percentage increase in productivity expected to stem from the training. A similar calculation should form the basis of the decision to train employees. If such an evaluation has not been made the measurement of productivity may benefit the organisation by prompting the need to undertake an analysis of some of their 'investments'. Further analysis may be undertaken regarding changes in employee remuneration over their life-cycle. If increased remuneration stems from increased training and/or experience the change in an employee's relative rate of remuneration may well provide an indicator of the change in relative marginal product. However, if wage increases are automatically linked to age and increases in age are believed to not reflect increased marginal products (possibly quite the opposite), then the weights should be adjusted accordingly. Needless to say, no value judgement is offered as to whether such a procedure **should** be identified as arguing for a wages policy related to marginal products; many other criteria impose on the use of age related salary scales in addition to short-term cost minimisation. It is only being argued that for the purpose of deriving weights for the measurement of labour input the above problems should be considered. Similarly, an apprentice in the final year of his or her training may well contribute an input of labour services only slightly below (or possibly equal to or more than) that of employees who have served their time. Relative wage rates may not reflect such a position and adjustments should be considered.

A model which attempts to incorporate quality changes in labour amenable to econometric estimation is outlined by Kennedy and Thirlwall [15]. The input of labour services is broken down into three parts: the growth of labour input in physical units; the average rate per annum of its improvement, λ_L; and the effect of changes in its average age,

$\lambda_L(\Delta e)$. The Cobb–Douglas production function, with constant returns to scale, embodying quality changes in labour input is given by:

$$O = A'(zL)^{\alpha}K^{\beta} \qquad \ldots (5)$$

where zL denotes labour input adjusted for quality changes and (for changes over discrete periods):

$$\frac{\Delta O}{O} = \frac{\Delta A'}{A'} + \beta\,\frac{\Delta K}{K} + \alpha\,\frac{\Delta L}{L} + \alpha\,\lambda_L - \alpha\,\lambda_L(\Delta\bar{e}) \qquad \ldots (6)$$

As Kennedy and Thirlwall note:

> "The two most important factors improving the quality of labour are the so-called learning process, which affects the average quality of labour, and education which may exert its effect both through changes in the average quality of labour and its "age" distribution if educational standards improve which benefit new workers." [15] p.37.

The above formulation may well improve the incorporation of changes in the 'quality' of labour into the measurement of labour input. However, the weighting of the contribution to production of different 'types' of labour according to relative 'prices' of such labour may again cause concern. Denison adopts this procedure as of necessity appreciating the compilation of that part of his labour input index which incorporates relative contributions of different sexes and age groups:

> " ... rests on the assumption that average earnings in the ten age-sex groups distinguished are proportional to the marginal products of labour, per hour worked, of these groups. If this assumption is correct, it is necessary and legitimate to consider an average hour worked by a demographic group whose average hourly earnings are twice as high as those of another group to represent twice as much labour input." [16]

Sex discrimination (pertaining to equal wages for equal work done as opposed to potential abilities), social norms, 'unequal' trade union pressure, non-monetary rewards, and many other such labour market 'imperfections' all serve to question the validity of this assumption [17].

For example, it may well be argued that the relatively higher wages paid to 'laggers' as compared with 'brickies' in the construction of a power station may not so much reflect the relative marginal products of the two groups of workers as opposed to the mopsonistic bargaining power of the former group. Whilst it is a relatively simple matter to point out such inconsistencies, the disentangling of the proportion of relative earnings associated with variations in marginal products is no easy matter, thus leaving us with this undesirable assumption. In recognising the need to give different weights to the changes in labour input of non-homogenous groups on the grounds that their marginal products differ, we must be careful not to introduce greater error by the use of relative earnings as an indicator of relative marginal products. Again, we must stress that the difficulties inherent in such decisions as to whether the relative earnings differential between, say, secretaries and line workers reflects relative marginal products usually lead to the use of relative earnings as weights in measures of labour input. For this reason we advocate the use of relative prices as the **basis** of the weighting system to be modified by informed adjustments.

Effort variation/labour hoarding

A further factor which merits concern is that the percentage utilisation of labour may vary within and between hours, say from paid labour hoarding. Thus for a homogenous group of employees man-hours worked may remain constant over time, yet the input of labour services may vary. Attempts have been made to incorporate such variations into the measurement of the input of labour services. Peak output per man-hour levels are identified and the observed output per man-hour as a proportion of the expected peak or potential level is noted. However, the input of capital services must be fully and accurately specified and removed in order to ensure that variations in capital usage, as opposed to labour usage, are not being identified [18].

Paid labour hoarding may take the form of labour spreading a lesser amount of work over a longer period and this under-utilisation of labour will be reflected in the above measure. Labour may also be put on short-time, the average number of hours worked per, say, year thus falling. Changes in the average number of hours worked per period would be reflected in the above measure and the reader may initially identify this as a correct representation for the input of labour would have correspondingly fallen. However, this need not be the case if the result of employees working, on average, shorter hours is to increase their marginal product during those hours and the result of employees working, on average, longer hours is to decrease their marginal products [19]. One may argue that in this latter case employers should hire more workers rather than increase the average working period. However, technological inflexibilities may preclude this; furthermore, hiring costs and national insurance contributions have to be incorporated into the price of 'new' labour as do expected demand patterns which, if believed to take the form of short-run cycles, may lead to firing costs. The aforementioned differences between the elasticities of output with respect to hours worked and number of employees in expression (1) reiterates the need for concern over the above.

Denison notes that:

> "The general shape of a curve relating hours to output for any given category of workers can be described with some assurance. If working hours are very long, the adverse effects of fatigue upon productivity are so great that output per worker increases if hours are shortened (and output per hour increases much more). The effects of fatigue are reinforced by a tendency for absenteeism, which is costly, to be excessive when hours are long, and by important institutional factors. If hours are shortened further, a point is reached below which output per hour continues to increase. At this stage, increases in output per hour only partially offset the reduction in hours worked. Finally, if hours worked become very short, the proportion of time spent in starting and stopping work may become so great that even output per hour declines as hours are shortened." [20]

In his study of the sources of growth between 1929 and 1969 Denison made assumptions concerning the relative "efficiency equivalent" of changes in hours worked by part-time workers; full-time non-farm wage and salary workers; full-time farm workers and full-time non-farm proprietors and unpaid family workers in the current year as compared with the preceding year. The principles upon which these quantitative estimates were made being given in the above quote [21].

Increased 'effort' by a given stock of labour will result in increased labour services, say through the adoption of a financial incentive scheme or greater participation in, and identification with, the organisation of the work process. For a particular organisation sudden shifts in production may be identified by a cumsum procedure [22] or incorporated ito a function via a dummy variable. Increases in the input of labour services may also stem from increases in the 'health' of the workforce, though indicators of the general health of the workforce are difficult to compile [23].

The accounting for variations in effort [24] expenditure is of importance since it represents a mechanism through which instantaneous adjustments in the productive powers of employees may be invoked. Promotion systems, transfers, disciplinary and supervisory practices, financial incentive schemes, may all be conceived of as management devices to control the input of effort from employees. Individual employees will react to a number of stimuli regarding effort expenditure in a number of ways, and the effort response will generally be sub-optimal as employees' personal goals (for example, a quiet life) conflict with organisational goals [25]. Payment by results schemes represent a device by which effort may be increased. They assume that such variation is possible (where rigid technological relationships dictate the pace of work such schemes may not be applicable) and that financial rewards are, and remain, substantively important to employees. For a piece-rate system individual employees are rewarded, at the margin, for increased rates of production. Yet the bonus rate for the increase in production not only relates to the additional production over and above a given level, but to ensuring the given level is attained after which the bonus is paid. In plant-wide schemes the marginal product of the average worker is considered.

Appraising the effectiveness of management techniques aimed at increasing effort begs the question of measuring changes in effort. Since effort cannot (at least practically) be measured directly the outcome of effort, that is, the productive manifestation ensuing from the variation in effort input, may be utilised. Labour productivity or output is an indirect indicator of effort. In a plant where capital service input, hours worked, in fact all factors aside from the effort put in by labour are held constant, as if frozen under a glass observation chamber in a controlled experiment, then the variation in effort by labour may be discerned by recourse to variations in output or labour productivity. Whilst a perfectly controlled (for other variables) experiment is not being mirrored in day to day industrial life, many of the variables can be isolated and identified as to whether they have changed. For example, a financial incentive scheme may be linked to labour productivity. Increases in production per man-hour worked (labour productivity) is assumed to stem from increased effort in turn stemming from the incentive of additional payments. Other variables which may affect this relationship include the input of capital services. Capital services would be generally expected to increase at a proportional rate conjoining with the increased labour input, machines working harder/quicker corresponding to labour's needs. However, if capital is substituted for labour, labour productivity will increase over and above that due to increased efforts, thus providing a bonus to employees not merited and rendering labour productivity to be a quite inadequate indicator of effort variability. Similarly, increased wear and tear on capital leading to less, or more haphazard and unreliable, capital services would lead to a fall in labour productivity quite unrelated to the desired effort, or physical and mental exertion, tedium, or fatigue re-organisation currently employed. However, if management believe that over the period in question, work re-organisation has not taken place, economies of scale not accrued, capital services not been adjusted to an extent not in accordance with increases in labour services, and other such factors have remained constant, output per man-hour worked may well provide a useful proxy indicator for effort variation. If, for example, capital services have varied to an extent over and above that required to meet increased effort input, then the increase in output not explained by capital service input may be derived from a properly specified production function estimated for the organisation. However, given a lack of statistical expertise by the organisation, estimation problems, existence of unstable coefficients over the reference period for which the time series was devised, such a procedure may not be practical.

Increased labour services may stem from an existing stock of labour if labour has been hoarded, that is, consciously under-utilised by management [26]. This may result from, say, a need to maintain skills, during short-run adverse fluctuations in demand, technical inflexibilities, and/or avoid hiring and firing costs. As the difference between potential services from labour available to an organisation during peak demand periods and actual services presently supplied, it can be estimated in terms of the difference between the productive manifestation of this effort in the above situations [27]. An estimate of potential labour productivity is derived from a time series of labour productivity data by fitting a linear trend through the peaks of such observations. It is assumed that labour is not being hoarded at these peak levels and an extrapolation of past peak levels will yield an estimate of future peak or potential labour productivity levels. The difference between observed labour productivity in a given period and expected potential productivity as an extrapolation from past peaks forms the basis of an estimate of labour hoarding [28]. The method, for reasons similar to those outlined for the measurement of effort variation, assumes the ratio of capital to labour services remains constant and no economies of scale or re-organisation of the work process has taken place. In such cases management may remove these effects through a 'guesstimate' as to the extent of such shifts caused by factors other than the increased utilisation of labour. In some cases, for example where a new machine has been purchased to be substituted for labour or re-organisation of the work process has been undertaken by a work study team, the guesstimate may be formed on a fairly sound basis (manufacturer's 'output' specification and work study team's evaluation). Alternatively, a production function may be estimated which incorporates these variables (preferably in a fully specified production function, though owing to estimation and measurement problems employment functions are often utilised in macro analysis)[29].

Finally, it may be argued that factors related to effort variation may also be related to morale. Morale is difficult to measure, though may well lead to effort variation especially where output related payment schemes and/or promotion paths do not exist or are not substantively effective. Pencavel [30] applied principal components analysis to the quit rate, accident rate, absenteeism rate and incidence of strike activity in order to derive a morale index for the coal industry. Principal components are artificial constructs combining inter-related variables. Whilst such a technique may not be generally applicable, the need to combine a range of factors which may denote the cause/effect of morale, as a useful explanatory factor for effort variation, merits attention.

Conclusion

Thus whilst we may conceptualise variations in the input of labour services, measurement is somewhat more difficult. A, say, chained Tornqvist index of weighted rates of growth of man—hours worked for a multitude of categories incorporating adjustments for under—utilisation, effort and so forth but marred by the empirical necessity to use relative labour prices in the weighting as opposed to marginal products becomes an attempt to measure an ideal. (However, if the reader feels 'short—changed' the next chapter brings further disappointments, for in the case of measuring capital services, there is some controversy as to whether the 'ideal' is even meaningful.) For labour input at the organisational level a starting point would be to classify labour by whatever variables noted above appear to be pertinent, say, 'type of work', skill level, experience, sex, whether undertaken in—house training. Having derived a table which provides the number of employees of each sub—group (undertaking a particular type of employment, of a particular skill, within a meaningful classificatory interval of experience — indicated by some weighted combination of pre—entry to the firm and period of time in that or related work in the firm — of a particular sex, having undertaken in—house training). For each sub—group of employees falling into a particular type of cell the relative employee remuneration should be given. Such a format should enable interaction effects to be isolated and marginal products derived as carried out by Chinloy [31]. However, the assumptions behind this process are fairly restrictive and the method requires some expertise.

At the micro level certain judgements may be made to possibly provide an acceptable indicator of labour input. First, the weights or relative employee compensation should reflect the relative marginal products of each 'cell' or sub—group of labour. Given perfect markets any discrepancy between this relationship should in the long run be corrected if the organisation is to remain competitive — this requires, however, a somewhat exaggerated belief in the effectiveness of market forces. In practice a manager may adjust the weights where a belief exists that the relative wages not so much reflect differences in marginal products stemming from skill differentials etc., but monopsonist powers of unions, tradition or discrimination (say, with respect to female employees). Such a procedure requires a judgement; yet this does not prejudice the method. Our aim is to discern changes in the services provided by labour. Whilst the dangers of having adjustments revealed to employees should be recognised, a framework is required that allows an (albeit) judgement that, for example, the marginal product of middle management relative to line workers can by no means be related to the relative price (compensation) of each group, to be incorporated. Such a judgement should be implicit in management decision making as to hiring of staff of different groups. Since the judgement is implicitly made in decisions of this type its incorporation as an attempt to explain variations in production should also be permissible.

Having derived weights for each cell these should not be applied directly to the change in the number of employees in each respective cell. Number of employees in each cell, for the two periods to be compared, should be converted to man-hours worked and experience or work studies set up to establish whether variation in input per employee occurs between different hours. Formally, hours overtime worked may be separately specified in a production function and the coefficient estimated [32]. Given estimation problems and a lack of such expertise, work study techniques may fulfil this task. Again such a procedure should be implicit in my judgement as to the employment of overtime work when compared with hiring new employees, plant, taking account of hiring costs and so forth. In deriving this framework an opportunity is provided to reconsider particular policy measures. Having derived changes in the flow of labour input for each cell the change may be combined using the Tornqvist formula (Chapter 3, equation (16)) with its assumption of a translog functional form and approximation properties to yield an indicator of labour input. Once established, the framework may be used to up-date the labour input 'account' on a regular basis, long run patterns being established through chaining. Differences between estimates of labour services supplied with and without adjustments or disaggregation reveal the effects of the variables being adjusted/aggregated for on labour input.

An example

The following example is intended to illustrate the operational side of the principles outlined in this chapter. It is highly simplified and, by its nature, cannot hope to match the features of all organisations. It is for the practioner to develop a suitable framework for their organisation utilising the principles outlined in this book, and this example as an illustration.

This example is concerned with the measurement of the change in labour input for a plant between periods 0 and 1;

Table 4.1

Number of employees, period 0

	A Trained	A Untrained	B Trained	B Untrained	Total
Male	5 800 / 740 740	3 480 / 444 310.8	15 3,000 / 2,640 2,640	2 400 / 352 281.6	25 4,680.0 / 4,176 3,972.4
Female	1 160 / 148 148	1 160 / 148 74	5 1,000 / 880 880	3 600 / 528 422.4	10 1,920.0 / 1,704 1,524.4
Subtotal	6 960 / 888 888	4 640 / 592 384.8	20 4,000 / 3,520 3,520	5 1,000 / 880 704	
Total	10 / 1,480.0	1,600.0 / 1,272.8	25 / 4,400.0	5,000.0 / 4,224.0	35 6,600.0 / 5,880 5,496.8

Type of Work

each period representing a month (4 weeks of 5 working days). Table 4.1 shows employees disaggregated by the 'type' of work they undertake, A or B, their sex and whether they are trained or untrained; a total of eight possible categories or 'cells'. Variables for disaggregation should include those which are believed to affect the flow of labour services per employee. Each cell is divided into four components. The top left component of each cell denotes the number of employees for that category. Thus, in period 0 there were 5 trained male employees undertaking type A work, 1 trained female employee undertaking type A work, 3 untrained female employees undertaking type B work and so forth. Table 4.2 is of the same format as Table 4.1, providing the corresponding information for period 1. Table 4.3 shows, for each cell and components within cells, the percentage change between period 0 and 1. Thus, the percentage change in the number of male, trained, type A employees is given by ((6–5) x 100)/5 = a 20.0 per cent increase. Table 4.3 also, for example, shows the number of untrained, male, type B employees to have **fallen** by 50 per cent and the number of trained, male, type B employees to have increased by 6.67 per cent.

Table 4.4 shows the relative importance of each category or cell of employees. Following the decision to apply the Tornqvist formula in Chapter 3 (formula 16) the relative importance or weight is calculated as the average (arithmetic mean) of relative labour remuneration in period 0 and period 1. The figures were adjusted by judgement if it was felt they more represent, say, bargaining strength, than relative marginal products or contribution of labour to output. Thus, although the number of male, untrained, type B employees fell by 50 per cent and the number of male, trained, type B employees increased by only 6.67 per cent (Table 4.3), the former (from Table 4.4) were given a weight of 3.7 per cent whilst the latter possessed a weight of 51.7 per cent, to a large extent reflecting the relatively larger number of employees in the latter group.

However, our concern lies not with changes in the stock or number of employees, but the flow of services they provide. The top right component of each cell in Tables 4.1, 4.2 and 4.3 provide the corresponding number of man–hours worked for each category of labour. In period 0 employees undertaking type A work each worked a standard month of 160 hours (40 hours per week). In period 1 this increased to 180 hours (45 hours per week) spread evenly between employees and days. In period 0 employees undertaking type B work each worked for 200

Table 4.2
Number of employees, period 1

Type of Work

	A		B		Total
	Trained	Untrained	Trained	Untrained	
Male	6 / 1,080 / 984 / 984	2 / 360 / 254 / 203.2	16 / 2,880 / 2,585.6 / 2,585.6	1 / 180 / 161.6 / 129.3	25 / 4,500 / 3,953.2 / 3,876.5
Female	1 / 180 / 166.4 / 166.4	1 / 180 / 166.4 / 83.2	6 / 1,080 / 969.6 / 969.6	3 / 540 / 484.8 / 387.8	11 / 1,980.0 / 1,787.2 / 1,607.0
Subtotal	7 / 1,260 / 1,150.4 / 1,150.4	3 / 540 / 388.4 / 260.8	22 / 3,960 / 3,555.2 / 3,555.2	4 / 720 / 646.4 / 517.1	36 / 6,480.0 / 5,740.4 / 5,483.5
Total	10 / 1,538.8	1,800.0 / 1,411.2	26 / 4,201.6	4,680.0 / 4,072.3	6,480.0 / 5,740.4 / 5,483.5

Table 4.3
Percentage change in labour input

| | Type of Work | | | | | | | | | |
| | A | | | | B | | | | Total | |
	Trained		Untrained		Trained		Untrained			
Male	20.0	35.0	-33.3	-25.0	6.67	-4.0	-50.0	-55.0	0	-3.85
	33.0	33.0	-42.8	-42.9	-2.1	-2.1	-54.1	-54.1	-5.3	-2.4
Female	0	12.5	0	12.5	20.0	8.0	0	-10	10.0	3.13
	12.4	12.4	12.4	12.4	10.2	10.2	-8.2	-8.2	4.9	5.4
Subtotal	16.67	31.25	-25.0	-15.6	10.0	-1.0	-20.0	-28.0		
	29.5	29.5	-34.4	-32.2	1.0	1.0	-26.5	-26.5		
Total	0		12.5		4.0		-6.4		2.86	-1.82
	4.0		10.9		-4.5		-3.6		-2.4	-0.24

Table 4.4

Weights based on adjusted relative labour remuneration

| | Type of Work | | | | |
| | A | | B | | |
	Trained	Untrained	Trained	Untrained	Total
Male	11.6	4.0	51.7	3.7	71.1
Female	2.1	1.1	18.4	7.4	29.0
Subtotal	13.7	5.1	70.1	11.1	
Total	18.8		81.2		100.0

* Weights are given by: $0.5(w_1 + w_0)$ as given by the Tornqvist formula (Chapter 3, formula (16)), where w is the relative remuneration being adjusted to better represent relative marginal products; expressed as a percentage.

hours per month (50 hours per week), this being reduced to 180 hours (45 hours per week) in period 1 spread evenly between employees and days. Thus, for the 5 trained male, type A employees, the number of man hours worked in period 0 (now equivalent to a month) was 5(160) = 800 hours, and in period 1, 6(180) = 1,080 hours; an increase of 35 per cent (Table 4.3). Thus, although the number of employees in this cell increased by 20 per cent the flow of man-hours worked increased by 35 per cent. This may be compared with type B employees where the pattern is in the opposite direction. If man-hours worked per employee varied within 'types' of work the corresponding conversion would, of course, be made from individual overtime absenteeism, sickness, late arrival records.

The bottom left component of each cell denotes a conversion of man-hours according to 'effort' variations. Assume that it has been noticed from monitoring output per employee (over periods when relative capital services and work organisaton and number of employees has been constant) that irrespective of the number of hours worked in the day, the first and last 3 hours of any week yield output per employee rates of one half the standard (non-overtime) level. This exists for trained and untrained employees irrespective of sex as if due to some socialisation phenomena. Furthermore, for male, type A employees (trained and untrained) the 20 hours overtime worked in period 1 is equivalent to 15 standard (average) hours worked, say due to fatigue. For female, type A employees (trained and untrained) the increased overtime of 20 hours was found to be equivalent to 18 standard hours. All type B employees worked 40 hours per month overtime in period 0 (over and above 160 hours per month) which was found to be equivalent to 25 standard hours; and 20 hours overtime in period 1, found to be equivalent to 12 standard hours. Finally, in period 1 an untrained, male, type A employee was on a work-to-rule and whilst he was paid at full-rate, a 'blind-eye' was turned to the fact that his labour services per man hour were a consistent half of the standard rate. (In practice we do not suggest such accounts should relate to individuals, the small numbers arising from our simplistic example.)

For male, trained, type A employees, period 0:

    man hours worked per employee, per month   = 160
    less, per employee, 12 hours, half rate for
        first and last 3 hours of each week   = 148
    for 5 employees = 148 x 5 = <u>740</u>

For male, trained, type A employees, period 1:

    man hours worked per employee, per month   = 180
    less, per employee, 6 hours, half rate for
        first 3 hours of each week   = 174
    less, loss of 4 hours per month being due to
        4 days per week of 16 hrs overtime worked
        at three-quarters efficiency   = 170
    less, 6 hours half-rate for the last 3 hours
        of each week   = 164
    for 6 employees = 164 x 6 = <u>984</u>

and so forth

The bottom right (and final) component of each category or cell includes an adjustment for 'experience'. We will assume for simplicity that when trained each employee possesses the same skill and experience, and no difference exists between male and female employees. The trained/untrained division refers to a three year training period. In the first year of training the contribution (from judgement and monitoring output) is one-half of a trained employee and in both the second and final year of training the contribution is 0.8 of a trained employee. In period 0 a single male and female untrained type A employee are in their first year of training and in period 1 only a female type A employee is in her first year of training. All other untrained employees are in their second or final year of training.

Thus, for trained employees the bottom left and right components of each cell remain the same. For untrained, male, type A employees, period 0, the adjustment is to: 148 (0.5) + 148 (0.8) + 148 (0.8) = 310.8. For untrained, male, type A employees period 1 the adjustment is to: 254 (0.8) = 203.2 and so forth. Increases are given in Table 4.3.

At this stage it is important to note the care with which the exercise should be conducted. Say, output variation per employee was also considered to stem from 'experience' in this type of activity. Now a school leaver undertaking the training scheme may well obtain 3 years specific experience. An employee hired with 3 years experience in another organisation undertaking similar work may well not possess skills of such a specific nature and, initially, his contribution may be slightly less. However, due to his experience in being able to propose alternative approaches, his contribution may be more than that directly measurable in terms of output. Similarly, output per employee, other things being equal, may vary with years of experience. Now a 'best fit' pattern to the relationship between output and experience may take the form of Figure 4.1 (though admittedly the step function for the training period is unusual, though introduced for simplicity alone). Following such a pattern employees with over 40 years of experience (assuming age and experience are perfectly correlated) will contribute rather less than trained younger employees, though the existence of age related salaries or equal rates in the absence of a piece rate system would not represent this. This is not to say that marginal criteria should be applied and the older employee replaced by a younger person (or wages reduced). The more experienced employee contributes by way of his/her experience possessing a knowledge of the organisation, customs, practices, contacts in different eventualities and so forth which is essential to the smooth running of the organisation. Invariably part of the training (formally or otherwise) falls under his/her auspices. Furthermore, the employee is also being rewarded for previous higher output levels when younger, an implicit understanding in the work contract being that the rate of services supplied may vary over the life-cycle of the contract. In addition, the greater flexibility of more experienced employees enables them to undertaken alternative tasks if required, their possessing a wider range of skills.

Yet the purpose of our measure is to account for productive changes between the two periods in question. If production, say, falls, as the workforce ages when recruitment is cut back then for this specific purpose adjustments may be required.

If this is the case, owing to the sensitivity of the issue, adjustments to aggregates should be made based on guesstimates. The mapping of individual performance as in Figure 4.1 is too dehumanising for the benefits that may accrue. It is true that piece rate systems actually concentrate on such differences in an attempt to isolate them and change them via financial incentives. The problem is that person A may well work at 1 and a quarter times the rate of person B in spite of person B's effort, because he is fitter, more skilled or whatever. Isolating this difference and incorporating it into the measure is conceptually valid **for this purpose**. Again, piece rate systems isolate and attempt to change via rewards such influences. Where such schemes are operating a data base exists to make adjustments for variations in the individual inputs in labour services or the same man—hour worked. The author appreciates that many managers may well see nothing 'wrong' with such a procedure. However, in the author's opinion such adjustments are best made as broad aggregates since, first, **changes** in effort variation between individuals is not expected to be of a significant magnitude and second, when effort variations do occur (say through the adoption of a plant—wide incentive scheme) they are more likely to represent 'shifts' in effort en masse, as opposed to changes between individuals thus being dealt with by an aggregate adjustment. This also removes the monitoring at a personal level which may add to discontent, and thus wastage, strike propensity, etc. As soon as we make decisions as to costs and benefits for profit maximisation there follows implications for the use of labour. The unique inflexibility labour can exercise through expressions of solidarity, absenteeism, lateness, etc., to curtail 'rational management' should be borne in mind by management.

However, in addition a normative statement may be made concerning the unique implications of treating labour as a resource for allocation, monitoring and modifying times and rates of input unrelated to the effectiveness of any response it can make. Management should be sensitive to the fact that they are responsible for monitoring and changing the life—styles of **people**. Isolating tendencies for a number of factors on aggregate to influence the flow of labour services should provide an opportunity to devise a strategy which best increases the flow of services per unit of labour whilst bearing in mind the above considerations.

Table 4.3 shows the percentage change in each component for

Figure 4.1

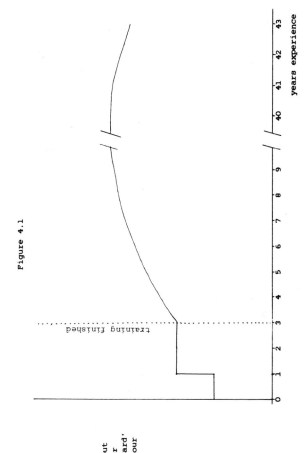

output
per
'standard'
man-hour

training finished

years experience

each cell between periods O and 1. Thus, for example, although employment of type B, trained male employees increased by 6.67 per cent, man hours worked fell by 4 per cent, though after adjusting for some 'dimensions of' effort variation, this amounted to a fall of only 2.1 per cent in the input of labour services. A similar analysis can be conducted for other cells bearing Table 4.4 in mind, which provides an indicator of the relative 'importance' of each category of employee. The totals given in Table 4.3 are a little artificial and may be misleading. Whilst total man-hours worked is meaningful, the indicators of the input of labour services are added together as if unit labour input from each category made an equal contribution to production changes. In fact, the very reasons for segregating employees by the variables sex, type of work, trained or not, was an a priori belief that an (adjusted) man hour worked in one category made a greater contribution than another. Practitioners should choose their own categories by recourse to a judgement as to which factors would be pertinent in accounting for such variation. The totals given in Table 4.3 assume no such between category variation to occur, an (adjusted) man-hour input from one category being equal to that from another.

Table 4.5 shows the weighted aggregation of changes in the input of man-hours for each category of labour using the Tornqvist formula for reasons outlined in Chapter 3. The weights are derived from Table 4.4 and the input of labour services for each category in periods O and 1 from Tables 4.1 and 4.2. The aggregate input of labour services to the organisation can be seen to have fallen by 0.821 per cent. Table 4.3 shows the sources of this change and Table 4.4 the relative importance of each source.

Table 4.5
The index of labour input

Source	Calculation[1]		
A; trained male	$0.116 \left[Ln \dfrac{984}{740} \right]$	=	0.03306
A; trained female	$0.021 \left[Ln \dfrac{166.4}{148} \right]$	=	0.00246
A; untrained male	$0.040 \left[Ln \dfrac{203.2}{310.8} \right]$	=	−0.01700
A; untrained female	$0.011 \left[Ln \dfrac{83.2}{74} \right]$	=	0.00129
B; trained male	$0.517 \left[Ln \dfrac{2,585.6}{2,640.0} \right]$	=	−0.01076
B; trained female	$0.184 \left[Ln \dfrac{969.6}{880} \right]$	=	0.01784
B; untrained male	$0.037 \left[Ln \dfrac{129.3}{281.6} \right]$	=	−0.02880

$$B; \text{untrained female} \quad \left[0.074 \left[\text{Ln} \, \frac{387.8}{422.4} \right] \right] = -0.00632$$

$$\text{Ln (index of labour input)} = -0.00824$$

Therefore, index of labour input = exp (−0.00824)

$$= 0.9918$$

ie. a **fall** of (1 − 0.9918)100 = 0.821 %

---

(1) $\text{Ln (index)} = \Sigma \, 0.5(w_1 + w_0)(\text{Ln } L_1 - \text{Ln } L_0)$

$$= \Sigma \, 0.5(w_1 + w_0) \left[\text{Ln } \frac{L_1}{L_0} \right]$$

Therefore, index $= \text{exp} \left[\Sigma \, 0.5(w_1 + w_0) \left[\text{Ln } \frac{L_1}{L_0} \right] \right]$

where: $0.5(w_1 + w_0)$ is the average (arithmetic mean) of the relative labour remuneration in periods 1 and 0 after adjustment as given in Table 4.4;

L_1 and L_0 is the labour input in periods 1 and 0 given in the bottom right square of each cell in Tables 4.1 and 4.2;   summation extends over sources or types of labour;

'Ln' is the natural logarithm of and 'exp' the exponent to the base 'e' of the expression following it.

1. Though real income per employee provides a quite different measure pertaining to changes in the benefits each employee generates a proportion of such benefits being directed to interest payments, taxes, depreciation, additions to capital stock and, of course, the employee directly in the form of changes in purchasing power.

2. Craine, R: "On the service flow from labour", Review of Economic Studies, January 1973.

3. Craine, ibid., 1973 and Wabe, J S: Problems in Manpower Forecasting, Saxon House, Farnborough, 1974, chapters 6 and 7, though see a more rigorous analysis in Leslie, D G and Wise, J: "The productivity of hours in UK manufacturing and production industries", Economic Journal, Vol.90, No.357, pp.716-815, March 1980.

4. Denison, E F: "Measurement of labour input: some questions of definition and the adequacy of data", in National Bureau of Economic Research, Output, Input and Productivity Measurement, Conference on Research in Income and Wealth, Studies in Income and Wealth, Vol.25, N.B.E.R, pp.347-386, 1961.

5. The formal derivation of this approach is given in Chinloy, P: "Sources of quality change in labour input", American Economic Review, Vol.70, No.1, March 1980.

6. Gollop, F M and Jorgenson, D W: "US productivity growth by industry, 1947-73", in J W Kendrick and B N Vaccara (eds.) New Developments in Productivity Measurement and Analysis, Studies in Income and Wealth, 44, University of Chicago and NBER, Chicago and London, 1980, see also Tachibanaki, T, who in a study of changes in labour input for Japanese manufacturing industry, incorporated the effects of changes in education, 'experience', age, sex and occupation into his measure of labour input ("Quality changes in labour input: Japanese manufacturing", Review of Economics and Statistics, August 1976. A similar study was undertaken for the US by Chinloy, P, op.cit., 1980.

7. See Jorgenson, D W and Griliches, Z: "The explanation of productivity change", <u>Review of Economic Studies</u>, Vol.34, 1967.

8. See Selowsky, M: "On the measurement of education's contribution to growth", <u>Quarterly Journal of Economics</u>, August 1969.

9. Doeringer, P B and Piore, M: <u>Internal Labour Markets and Manpower Analysis</u>, Heath, Lexington D.C., 1971, and Ziderman, A: <u>Manpower Training: Theory and Policy</u>, Macmillan, London, 1978.

10. Oatey, M: "The economics of training with respect to the firm", <u>Journal of Industrial Relations</u>, March 1970.

11. See Denison, E F (assisted by Poullier, J P): <u>Why Growth Rates Differ: Postwar Experience in Nine Western Countries</u>, Brookings Institution, Washington, 1977, Chapters 8 and 9 and Denison, E F, <u>Accounting for United States Economic Growth, 1929-1969</u>, Brookings Institution, Washington, 1974.

12. Becker, G: <u>Human Capital: A Theoretical and Empirical Analysis with Special Reference to Education</u>, National Bureau of Economic Research, New York, 1964.

13. See Eckhaus, R S: "Investment in human beings: a comment", <u>Journal of Political Economy</u>, Oct.1968, and Oatey, M: "The economics of training with respect to the firm", <u>British Journal of Industrial Relations</u>, 1970.

14. See Heckman, J J: "Estimates of a human capital production function embedded in a life-cycle model of labour supply" in N E Terleckyj (ed.) <u>Household Production and Consumption</u>, Conference on Research in Income and Wealth, <u>Studies in Income and Wealth</u>, Vol.40, National Bureau of Economic Research, New York, 1975, with comment by Schultz, pp.227-259.

15. Kennedy, C and Thirlwall, A P: "Technical progress: a survey", <u>Economic Journal</u>, Vol.82, March 1972.

16. Denison, op.cit., 1974, p.33.

17. See Pen, J: <u>Income Distribution</u>, Penguin, Harmondsworth, 1974, pp.94-113, for a discussion of

these and further points.

18. For details see Evans, G J: "The labour markeet mechanism and the hoarding of manpower", in Wabe, op.cit., Chapter 5; Fair, R C: The Short Run Demand for Workers and Hours, North Holland Publishing Co., Amsterdam, 1969; Taylor, J: "The behaviour of unemployment and unfilled vacancies; Great Britain, 1958-71. An alternative view", Economic Journal, 1972.

19. For a study of the marginal productivity of overtime see Leslie, D G and Wise, J: "The productivity of hours in UK manufacturing and production industries", Economic Journal, Vol.90, No.357, March 1980, pp.74-85.

20. Denison, 1974, op.cit., p.38.

21. For further details: ibid, pp.38-41; Denison, op.cit., 1967, pp.59-64.

22. See Lewis, C D: "The automatic detection of discontinuities in 'noisy' time-series data", University of Aston Management Centre Working Paper Series, No.147, 1979.

23. See Denison, 1967, op.cit., p.114 and Appendix G for discussion of the lack of effect on US postwar economic growth of changes in calorie intake as established by: Cosrea, H and Cummins, G: "Contribution of nutrition to economic growth", American Journal of Clinical Nutrition, Vol.23, May 1970.

24. See Mangan, J: "The intra-organisational flow of labour services" in J Edwards et al, Manpower Planning: Strategies and Techniques at the Organisational Level, J. Wiley, London, 1983.

25. Liebenstein, H: "Allocative efficiency vs. X-efficiency", American Economic Review, June 1966.

26. Taylor, J: "The theory and measurement of labour hoarding: a comment", Scottish Journal of Political Economy, 1979.

27. Mangan, J: "On the measurement of labour hoarding", University of Aston Manaagement Centre Working Paper Series, No.176, March 1980.

28. See Taylor, op.cit., 1979.

29. Miller, R L: "The reserve labour hypothesis: some tests of its implications", Economic Journal, 1971, pp.17-35.

30. Pencavel, J H: "An index of industrial morale", British Journal of Industrial Relations, 1974.

31. Chiloy, P, op.cit., 1980.

32. See Leslie, D G and Wise, J, op.cit., 1980.

5 The input of capital services

The Cambridge Controversy

In her introduction to a seminal article on the measurement of capital Prof. Joan Robinson noted that:

> " ... the production function has been a powerful instrument of miseducation. The student of economic theory is taught to write $0 = f(L,C)$ where L is a quantity of labour, C a quantity of capital and 0 a rate of output of commodities. He is instructed to assume all workers alike, and to measure L in man-hours of labour; he is told something about the index-number problem involved in choosing a unit of output; and then he is hurried on to the next question, in the hope that he will forget to ask in what units C is measured. Before ever he does ask, he has become a professor, and so sloppy habits of thought are handed on from one generation to the next." [1]

The problem arises from what we shall label as the 'Cambridge Criticism' of 'neo-classical' theory explaining factor prices (and rewards) by reference to the marginal products of such factors [2]. Aggregation problems have long been recognised in production function work [3], however criticisms of capital measurement no longer relate to restrictive assumptions but to the very meaning of "capital" as a factor of production.

For a given equilibrium position the 'quantity' of capital represents physical stocks of equipment or instruments of production. Capital is also a source of income for those who own these stocks or instruments of production. A problem arises as to whether a unit of measurement exists for aggregate capital which simultaneously performs both functions. The 'quantity' of capital requires aggregating quantities of specific capital goods with differing techniques embodied, of differing qualities, ages, etc. The element of time rules out aggregation of physical capital stock, since capital is a heterogeneous collection of goods resulting from past decisions and prices. To aggregate such a stock in money terms requires a knowledge of the price of capital, or rate of interest. Thus:

" ... neo-classical theory gets into a vicious circle of explaining capitalists' incomes by assuming a given value of capital which can only be explained if capitalists' incomes are known." [4]

The marginal productivity of capital cannot be shown to determine the rate of interest since to ascertain the 'quantity' of capital (and thus its marginal product) we need to know the rate of interest. The same stock of capital would aggregate to different values with every variation in the rate of interest. The 'Cambridge Criticism' has been strengthened by the discovery of 'double-switching' and 'capital reversion', the former being that the same technique of production may be competitive both at relatively high and low rates of interest and may be dominated by a different technique for values of the rate of interest between the two. Capital reversion notes that lower capital intensity may arise from lower values of the rate of profit as opposed to leading to a higher capital intensity [5].

In an attempt to surmount these difficulties neo-classical theory treats capital as being reducible to some primary substance ranging from meccano sets [6] to putty, jelly and butter. Alternatively, each capital good is treated as an alternative factor in terms of dated labour or commodities, yet this still implies a price which leads to the aforementioned circular argument. 'Surrogate' capital is used [7] to avoid the problem of double switching by assuming a uniform capital-labour ratio in all sectors, yet this hardly leads to an explanatory model. Champernowne arranged all alternative methods of production into a 'chain' such that any two consecutive techniques in the chain are equally profitable for a given rate of profit. Yet the case fails to 'explain' double-switching and implies the rate of profit is independent (in that it is given) [8].

Denison simply justified the use of relative factor earnings as weights for changes in factor inputs by recourse to neo-classical theory.

"The total earnings of each factor can be viewed as equal to the number of units of the factor and its price, or earnings, per unit. The marginal product of each factor is the extra output that would be added by one additional unit of that factor when the quantities of the other factors are held constant. If enterprises combine the ... factors in such a way as to minimise costs they will use them in such proportions that the marginal products per unit of the several factors are proportional to their prices, or earnings, per unit. Unless this condition is satisfied, enterprises could reduce costs by substituting one factor for another. Departures from this situation are assumed to be small or offsetting so that total earnings of the ... inputs are proportional to the number of units of each times its marginal products." [9]

The above, whilst causing some economists to 'wince', did not deter economists in this area. This is not to say that such economists were unconcerned with aggregation problems for the production function as witnessed by greater refinement from Solow [10] and Jorgenson and Griliches [11]. However, the basic framework remains.

Our purpose, however, is not to derive the rate of return to capital from measures of the marginal productivity of capital. It arises from a recognition that capital increases the productive powers of labour and thus must figure in any framework relating to 'sources of growth'. The concern with capital reversion and double switching arose, as argued by Sen [2], from different considerations. Our aggregation arises from a pragmatic need to ascertain the extent to which capital services are changing rather than relying, with its many more imperfections, on the judgements of managers or decisions implicit in the status quo. Detailed financial analysis may form the basis for decisions as to the purchase of new machinery, etc. Yet to say, for example, that labour productivity is increasing for the organisation begs the question as to trends in the aggregate change in capital services. The aggregation problems warn us about conceptual problems in interpretation and inaccuracies in estimates of the service flow of capital. As may be apparent from the following discussion, our focus on changes in service characteristics which are possible to estimate at the micro level goes some way to minimising such problems.

We must now turn to what must be stressed is an **attempt** to reflect changes in the input of capital services. It is worth noting that for macro studies our attempts to represent such changes are based on restrictive assumptions. Some adjustments to improve these estimates require a detailed knowledge of each organisation/industry which is rarely possessed by economists. At the level of the organisation such adjustments may be made with somewhat more conviction. Some economists may be satisfied with changes in the deflated value of capital stock as an indicator of capital services provided by, say, sewing machines, in a company. The manager of a company may possess details of the number of stitches per minute of more up—to—date machines whose real capital cost is the same as old machines, and adjust the measure of input of capital services accordingly. Thus, by comparing adjusted and non—adjusted flows of capital services the effect of embodied technological progress can be discerned. Part of the answer lies with knowing what is required of our measure, another part with data and the last with the genuine inability to aggregate heterogeneous capital into meaningful units of measurement.

The Measurement of the Input of Capital Services

The perpetual inventory method

Consider a tailoring establishment which utilises sewing machines and clothes presses. In order to arrive at an aggregate measure of the capital stock we must assume that the relative prices reflect the relative (marginal) contribution of the two capital goods (these being independent of labour). Our starting point must be to look to the inadequacies of changes in the gross value of capital stock as an indicator of the flow of capital services.

Consider the value of capital stock at the beginning of a period as the sum of each 'type' of capital good multiplied by its price, p. Where there are $k_{t,i}$ ($i = 1, 2, \ldots n$) capital goods of type i, for the beginning of period t, the total value of capital stock, K_t, is given by:

$$K_t = p_{t,1}k_{t,1} + p_{t,2}k_{t,2} + p_{t,3}k_{t,3} + \cdots p_{t,n}k_{t,n}$$

$$\ldots (2)$$

Additions to this stock over the period t are given by gross investments, $I_{t,i}$ for each type of capital good (i = 1, 2, ...n). Any fall—off in capital services over the period t is represented, by some rule, by depreciation for each capital good, denoted by $D_{t,i}$. Thus the change in the value of capital stock in period t is given by:

$$\Delta K_{t,i} = I_{t,i} - D_{t,i} \qquad \ldots (3)$$

The value of capital stock in any period is given by the value in an initial period (computed by an adaptation of this method) plus additions to and subtractions from the stock in each respective period. Thus, for a time series of the value of capital stock this method (the perpetual—inventory method) yields:

$$K_{t,i} = K_{0,i} + \sum_{j=0}^{t-1} \Delta K_{j,i} \qquad \ldots (4)$$

The deflation of capital

In order to measure changes in capital input over time the effects of price changes need to be removed, since it is the real (physical volume of) capital input that concerns us, not simply a, say, increase in gross capital stock owing to the effects of inflation. Appropriate price indexes must be compiled for the organisation which reflect changes in the prices of purchased capital. Yet, care must be exercised in the treatment of quality changes. If the price of a machine in one year increases solely because it is a better machine, the deflation of the cost of capital by an index which incorporates this price change will remove from the deflated measure of capital stock the effect of these quality changes. Since the purpose of our measure is to represent changes in the services supplied by capital, this is not desirable. Attempts must be made to remove from the price indexes used any component associated with quality changes. Such estimates may be feasible at the organisational level given the purchaser's special knowledge. It may be difficult to disentangle the effects of 'general' price rises from quality related ones, but some attempt is better than the bias which would result if no attempt was made at all. It is important to bear in mind the purpose of the exercise is to represent the flow of capital services. Even if the price of a much improved piece of equipment remains constant the 'price' deflator would have to incorporate a notional fall to allow the quality change to be registered.

An alternative approach is to directly apply the Tornqvist quantity formula given in Chapter 3, equation (16). For a 'type' of capital the change in its services is estimated, preferably by recourse to a meaningful characteristic, say productive ability per hour, or some invariant combination of characteristics similar to that discussed under hedonic indices in Chapter 2. The weight attached to each machine by necessity is given by the relative cost of the machines as given in the weighting component of the Tornqvist formula. If management believe the relative price of one piece of capital may not relate to its marginal product, say, because of monopolistic power on the part of a capital goods manufacturer, or cut-prices through bulk purchases or some form of economies of scale, then the weight may be adjusted by a 'guesstimate'. The Tornqvist index should be chained regularly in order to take account of variations in the relative input of different 'types' of capital [12].

Utilisation, wear and tear

Since we are concerned with the services a stock of capital provides, variations in the utilisation of a given stock of capital must be taken into account and the input of capital appropriately adjusted. This is particularly necessary if variations in the number/length of shifts take place or where production is not evenly distributed over the reference period, say for the seasonal demand for a product with a low or expensive storage life [13]. In the short-run capital utilisation may vary with demand fluctuations [14]. At the organisational level accurate data may be collected on the utilisation of capital stock, say in terms of variations in machine-hours worked as a proportion of a 'standard' working period.

It should be noted that at the macro level a range of techniques have been devised in order to ascertain the extent of capacity utilisation. These range from utilising the difference between extrapolations of peaks in output and actual output to the specification of production functions with capital and labour input estimated at their peak levels (usually by recourse to establishing time series from peaks of these variables) [15]. An alternative procedure is to utilise fluctuations in the power or fuel as an indicator of capital capacity utilisation [16]. A knowledge of the technological features of the production process should indicate whether such an indicator is appropriate. Experience of the manufacturer of the capital goods may enable the derivation of full capacity fuel/power levels and the pattern of the relationship (if, for example, linear, and if so the fixed element and the slope coefficient – these may be derived from regression analysis). Alternatively, the degree of utilisation may be simply a matter of timing the number of hours a machine is utilised, or timing multiplied by some indicator of 'speed' of operation – say utilised at x per cent of full possible services for y per cent of the time. Adjustments may be made accordingly.

Even if the capital stock is being utilised at a constant rate over time, as capital ages, so too might its productive ability. Standard accounting provisions for depreciation are unlikely to reflect the 'wear and tear' or deterioration of capital with respect to the services it provides [17]. Denison, appreciating the need to allow for deterioration of capital and maintenance costs (which are excluded from net output) utilises a weighting procedure since straight–line depreciation provisions are (implicitly) believed to overestimate the deterioration; he uses:

" ... a weighted average of the indexes of the gross stock and net stock based on straight–line depreciation, with the gross stock weighted three and the net stock one ... The procedure implies that, on average, a capital good with one–half of its useful service life exhausted can contribute seven–eighths as much to net–output (when net output itself is measured by use of straight–line depreciation and after deduction of maintenance costs) as an otherwise identical good that is unused, and three–fourths as much shortly before its retirement." [18]

Whilst the use of assumed average depreciation patterns may be acceptable at the macro level owing to data limitations, at the micro level the effect of wear and tear on the services provided by a machine should be discerned. In many cases, the services provided by a machine throughout its life may well be almost constant (assuming servicing and repair). In any event, the likely pattern may be determined from experience and recourse to the manufacturer of the capital goods. Such information should have been considered in the decision to purchase the capital good.

Given that the physical flow of services from a type of capital good can be adjusted for wear and tear (breakdowns, decreased 'performance' in terms of units produced or quality of goods produced and higher reject rate in quality control), consideration must be given to the relative importance of the machine when aggregating with other capital goods and labour. The deflation process can be achieved by considering weighted changes in physical quantity relatives, that is the weight multiplied by change in services. We have argued in Chapter 3 that the weights should be adjusted regularly via the chained method. Consider a tailoring firm with 4 sewing machines all 3 years old. A new sewing machine identical to existing ones is purchased increasing the flow of capital services by 20 per cent. The, say, six tailors employed for manufacturing and repairing of wearing apparel now have 20 per cent more capital services, no longer needing to remain idle, as previously, whilst awaiting use of machine for non-manual tasks. The relative importance of capital (sewing machine) services has increased. Now the weighting of machines to labour should reflect this. One course of action is to consider all machines as not being equal. Whilst they produce the same capital services, since one machine is new, it has a longer economic life than the other machines. As such, it should be valued as being worth more. Such a procedure is outlined by Faucett [19]. Each year existing stock loses one year of its remaining life and its value should be adjusted accordingly. However, our purpose is to reflect the contribution to production of capital via its weight and real increase. The real increase in capital services is 20 per cent, the weight of capital relative to labour we will assume is given by the relative cost of capital to labour. For our purpose there is no need to depreciate the value of the older machines by a proportion equivalent to their economic life, since given labour costs are not being diminished relative to the proportion of their life served, the relative importance of the old machines to labour has not diminished in terms of contributing to output. In this context the new machine should be valued at the same relative weight as an old machine, since its contribution as a source of production via the technical relationship between the factors of production and output is the same. There will come a point in time when an existing machine finishes the end of its natural life or is retired out. The weight, relative importance of its contribution to the production process, becomes zero. If the old machines perform at a, say, gradually diminishing rate over time, then the extent of this should be monitored/ estimated via past experience and capital goods manufacturer's specifications. Thus, the flow of real services can be adjusted as can the weight. An old machine is in this instance not as important as a new machine, not because of having lived a proportion of its natural life, but because its flow of productive services has diminished, it has become less important as a source of, or contribution to, production changes. It is important to distinguish between obsolescence and capital deterioration. Obsolescent capital can contribute to production and if depreciation provisions are based on an expected age related to obsolescence, depreciation will be over-estimated.

Technical change

Having adjusted the stock of capital for utilisation and wear and tear to provide a better indicator of the flow of capital services, we now return to the problem that the quality of capital may change over time, and thus, the flow of services from it, as it is replaced by new capital incorporating technical improvements. We first examine the incorporation of technical change in econometric studies. We consider two forms of technical change. Disembodied technical change assumes no investment is necessary to take advantage of technical progress, that is, the 'efficiency' of capital (and labour) grows at a similar and externally given rate, say λ% per annum. Thus, the Cobb-Douglas production function, as first specified by Tinbergen [20] incorporating disembodied technical change is given by:

$$Q = AL^{\alpha} K^{\beta} e^{\lambda t} \qquad \qquad \ldots (5)$$

Solow [21] subsequently suggested that technological change may be embodied in new machines (though 'organisational technological change' is specified externally) and all ages or vintages of capital may not share equally in technological progress. The more recent additions to the capital stock embodying technological change may generate a greater input of capital services than 'similar' preceding inputs of capital [22].

Embodied technological progress has been incorporated into a Cobb-Douglas production function by Nelson [23], as given by:

$$Q_t = A_t^1 \, L^\alpha \, J_t^\beta \qquad \qquad \ldots (6)$$

where A_t^1 represents technological progress excluding improvements in the quality of capital;

and J_t is the quality weighted number of machines with new machines giving greater weight than old machines.

If we assume that technological progress allows for increases in the 'quality' of machines at 100λ per cent per annum,

$$J_t = \sum_0^t K_{vt} (1 + \lambda)^v \qquad \qquad \ldots (7)$$

where k_{vt} is the gross amount of capital in year v, that is of vintage v, which is in use at time t.

For a Cobb-Douglas production function with constant returns to scale ($\alpha + \beta = 1$):

$$0 = A \, L^\alpha \, J^\beta \qquad \qquad \ldots (8)$$

and for discrete changes after taking logarithms and differentiating with respect to time:

$$\frac{\Delta 0}{0} = \frac{\Delta A}{A} + \alpha \, \frac{\Delta L}{L} + \beta \, \frac{\Delta J}{J} \qquad \qquad \ldots (9)$$

and, with embodied technological change, taking a similar form to the incorporation of 'quality' changes in labour outlined in Chapter 4:

$$\frac{\Delta 0}{0} = \frac{\Delta A}{A} + \alpha \, \frac{\Delta L}{L} + \beta \, \frac{\Delta K}{K} + \beta\lambda - \beta\lambda(\Delta\bar{a}) \qquad \ldots (10)$$

where Δa is the change in the average age of capital and thus an indicator of the change in the gap between the average level of technology and the 'best practice technology';

λ may have to be estimated on a 'trial and error' basis with respect to finding the best fit for the model.

The above specification is an attempt to incorporate embodied technical change in a form such that the production function can be estimated. The last term in equation (9) has been decomposed into three parts given, in turn, by the last three terms in equation (10); the growth in the actual capital stock; the average rate of its improvement; the effect of changes in its average age (which is a function of changes in the rate of investment).

There have been some critics of the embodied model, and estimated functions based on embodied technical progress have not always performed as well, in terms of explaining growth, as estimates based on disembodied technological progress. Empirical results are, however, somewhat conflicting [24]. At the micro level, firms may test econometrically both the embodied and disembodied models for explanatory power, though an insight into the nature of the production process may well provide an initial hypothesis. The incorporation of both types of technological progress in a single model may be attempted, though it is likely that one may be faced with the statistical problem of multicollinearity.

However, at the micro level embodied technological change may be incorporated directly into the indicator of capital services. If the services of a particular capital good can best be expressed in terms of a performance characteristic and the technological advance takes the form of an increase in this characteristic then an adjustment may be incorporated. For example, consider a factory where the existing stock of n sewing machines provides for x stitches per hour; an old machine is retired and a new one purchased at the same real cost, but being able to produce y stitches per hour instead of x/n stitches for the retired machine. The increase in total capital services is: $[(x-x/n)+y]/x$. However, if the new machine can also cope with more tasks, say types of stitches, than the other machines the proportion of time spent on each task may be isolated for this machine. The flow of capital services for all sewing machines may then be decomposed into the different performance characteristics and aggregated for all machines. The combination of the different character-istics requires some weighting procedure. In this instance time spent on each type of stitching operation may be appropriate if one component (type of stitch) of the capital may be regarded as being as equally important as another. If one stitch is particularly complicated, this being reflected in a significant increase in the price of machines with this facility, relative to those with other facilities, then the

additional relative price of this facility and a judgement as
to the use derived in the production process, may be utilised
to adjust the weighting of the different characteristics.
Needless to say, further complications can arise as organisations employ capital with many performance characteristics,
some increasing labour productivity by substituting for
labour, some simply enhancing the productive powers of labour
maintaining a constant capital (stock) to labour ratio. In
many cases management/employee estimates may have to be made;
however, it is hoped that the framework given will provide
some guidance. Eventually a matrix of 'types' of capital with
weights and increase in services may be derived. Adjustments
for utilisation and wear and tear are made and upon aggregation yield an estimate of the input of capital services. In
some industries the aggregation problems and establishment of
performance characteristics may be quite straightforward. In
others multiple characteristics may necessitate the
derivation of 'price' estimates for each characteristic by
recourse to the regression coefficient of an hedonic
relationship as outlined in Chapter 2. However, by reducing
the problem to one of discerning the flow of capital services
and identifying performance characteristics as an appropriate
indicator(s) of such a flow at least the direction of our goal
is provided.

Having considered some attempts to measure changes in the
input of capital services, it is worth summarising some of the
points made. Partial measures of productivity serve specific
functions but cannot tell the whole story. It is possible to
conceive of a framework whereby if changes in the input of
labour and capital services were properly measured changes in
real production would be accounted for, in the sense that such
changes would be made up of the appropriately weighted
relative contribution of changes in each factor input. If
quality changes are not incorporated into the measurement of
factor inputs such quality changes may be represented by an
exponential time trend. However, such quality changes (or
technical progress) may favour specific factor inputs or be
'neutral'. Hicks [25], in trying to explain the broad
historical consistency of distributive shares, considered a
neutral definition as one which, with given factor
proportions, raised the marginal product of labour in the
same proportion as the marginal product of capital. Harrod
[26], on the other hand, being concerned with the development
of a theory of equilibrium growth, defined technical progress
as neutral if, with a constant rate of interest it left the
capital output ratio unchanged. For a Cobb–Douglas

production function disembodied neutral technical change will, thus, have no effect on relative factor proportions.

Non-neutral technical change may take several forms depending on the definition of neutrality considered and whether it saves or augments capital, labour, inputs or products. Without considering this issue in detail what we should note is that changes in the capital to labour ratio may not only stem from relative factor prices (amongst other variables), but also from labour or capital saving bias in technical progress. In practice the two effects are difficult to disentangle [27].

Measurement problems will undoubtedly preclude us from fully accounting for changes in output by reference to changes in inputs. Measurement errors would include those arising from the marginal rates of transformation not being equal to relative factor prices both between factors and within types of factors (and not being independent of the 'other' factor) and such errors not offsetting each other; failure to adjust for utilisation of capital and labour or adjust for changes in 'effort' by labour; the effects of economies or dis-economies of scale; the effects of shifts in resources between sectors and within sectors not being properly accounted for [28]; and a host of qualitative influences.

If 'quality' changes are regarded as being embodied in capital we may attempt to incorporate such changes as described above. Yet our attempt will remain imperfect and the residual term may well subsume all other effects with measurement errors and spurious associations rendering interpretation in explanatory terms a somewhat heroic step.

Total factor productivity becomes an important concept arising from the inability of partial measures to fully explain growth. It is only natural that economists have spent time and resources in an attempt to fully explain the contributions of factors, technical progress, variation in utilisation, economies of scale, etc. to growth. This religious search has become even more important given the neo-classical theoretical link between relative (marginal) contributions and relative factor incomes. Yet it has been argued that the assumptions behind the basic framework and measurement problems may well place the 'Grail' beyond reach. A related approach is to treat it as a theoretical construct and attempt to derive estimates of the source of production changes, acknowledging some measurement, aggregation errors. By a process of re-adjusting elementary indicators by recourse to management, employees, capital goods manufacturers' estimates and experience an insight may be gained. Since much decision-making implicitly requires these estimates such a procedure is likely to be an improvement on assumptions implicit in 'continuing as before' or 'rough' judgements.

Any residual or unexplained output variation may not be automatically ascribed to economies of scale, reorganisation of the work process or disembodied technological change. If work study has resulted in a reorganisation of the work process then the effects of this, or a means by which it can be monitored, should form part of the work study package. By considering areas from which economies or diseconomies of scale may stem estimates of their possible effects may be judged, at least within an interval range. Approximation errors referred to throughout this book and the use of labour and capital compensation as measures of 'relative importance' constrain the extent to which meaning can be given to the residual. Yet unaccounted for sources of growth, if significant, are at least worth establishing in case the reservoir has not been fully tapped. In this instance, little guidance can be given for such sources can be discerned only by recourse to the individual characteristics of the establishment. Management, foremen, employees have a unique role to play in this area which macro studies cannot emulate. Changes in, say, flexibility of work practices, fall-offs in morale over particular issues, can all be identified at the organisational level in an aim to account for, and subsequently influence, contributions to production changes and, thus, productivity.

NOTES

1. Robinson, J: "The production function and the theory of capital", Review of Economic Studies, Vol.21, 1953-4; the omission of land from the production function in the quote is footnoted in the article for the purpose of simplifying her subsequent discussion.

2. An excellent summary of the debate and collection of the major articles are contained in Harcourt, G C and Laing, N F (eds.), Capital and Growth, Penguin, Harmondsworth, 1971. Our outline is by necessity very brief and hardly does justice to the standard of the debate. The reader interested in this area is well recommended to consult the above. A more recent survey is given by Ranadive, K R: Income Distribution, The Unsolved Puzzle, Oxford University Press, Bombay, 1978, Chapter IV, and for an amusing article see Sen, A, "On some debates in capital theory", Economica, Vol.41, August 1974. Some of the criticisms were recognised by 'neo-classical' economists, see Wicksell, J G K, Lectures on Political Economy, Routledge and Kegan Paul, London, (1901) 1934, Vol.I, pp.149-57.

3. For a summary see Ranadive, op.cit., Chapter IV and Diewert, W E: "Aggregation problems in the measurement of capital", in Dan Usher (ed.), The Measurement of Capital, National Bureau of Economic Research, Studies in Income and Wealth, 45, University of Chicago Press, Chicago and London, NBER, 1980.

4. Pen, J: Income Distribution, Penguin, Harmondsworth, 1971, p.418.

5. For details see Readings by Samuelson, Bhaduri, and Painetti in Harcourt and Laing, op.cit., part 5, and Garegnani, P: "Heterogeneous capital, the production function and the theory of distribution", Review of Econonic Studies, vol.37, 1970.

6. Swan, T W: "Economic growth and capital accumulation", Economic Record, Vol.32, 1956.

7. SOmuelson, P A: "Parable and realism in capital theory: the surrogate production function", Review of Economic Studies, Vol.39, 1962.

8.   Champernowne, D G: "The production function and the theory of capital: a comment", Review of Economic Studies, Vol.21, 1953-4;   see also Brown, M: "The measurement of capital aggregates: a postreswitching problem", in Dan Usher (ed.), 1980, op.cit.

9.   Denison, E F: Accounting for United States Economic Growth, 1920-1969, Brookings Institution, Washington, 1974, p.51.

10. Solow, R M: "Technical progress and productivity change", Review of Economics and Statistics, Vol.39, 1957.

11. Jorgenson, D W and Griliches, Z: "Explanation of productivity change", Review of Economic Studies, Vol.34, 1967.

12. See Jorgenson and Griliches, ibid., and Griliches, Z and Jorgenson, D W: "Sources of measured productivity change: capital input", American Economic Association, Papers, May 1966.   For a discussion of appropriate price deflators see Gordon, R J: "Measurement bias in price indexes for capital goods", Review of Income and Wealth, Series 17, No.2, June 1971 and Denison, E F, Griliches, Z and Jorgenson, D W: "The measurement of productivity", Survey of Current Business, Special issue, Vol.52, May 1972 and Chapter 3.

13. See Winston, G C: "On measuring factor proportions in industries with different seasonal and shift patterns or did the Leontief paradox ever exist?" Economic Journal, Vol.89, December 1979.

14. Omission of an adjustment for utilisation will leave the effects included in the residual or total factor productivity along with such effects as increasing returns to scale, technological progress not included in the measurement of capital input, etc.   Denison, E F, op.cit., does not adjust capital for utilisation but examines its effects as one of the contributions to fluctuations in 'output' divided by total factor input (chapter 6).

15. For a survey of methods see Briscoe, G, O'Brian, P, and Smyth, O J: "The measurements of capital utilisation in the United Kingdom", Manchester School, June 1970;

Klein, L R and Preston, R S: "Some new results in the measurement of capacity utilisation", American Economic Review, March 1967; Hazledine, T and Watts, I: "Short-term production functions and economic measures of capacity for UK manufacturing industries", Oxford Bulletin of Economic Statistics, Vol.39, 1978, pp.273-289.

16. See Foss, M: "The utilisation of capital equipment", Survey of Current Business, Vol.43, 1963.

17. Young, A H and Musgrave, J C: "Estimation of capital stock in the United States", in Dan Usher, 1980, op.cit., pp.23-83, have argued that straight line depreciation may provide viable estimates given that some effects may be offsetting the resulting pattern taking this form. However, see comments by Rymes and Faucett to this point following the paper.

18. Denison, op.cit., p.55.

19. See comment to Young and Musgrave's article, in Dan Usher, 1980, op.cit., by Faucett.

20. Tinbergen, J: "Zur theorie der langfristigen wirtschaftsentwicklung", Weltwirschaftliches Archiv, May 1942.

21. Solow, R M: "Investments and economic growth: some comments", Productivity Measurement Review, November 1959.

22. See Kennedy and Thirlwell, op.cit.; Johansen, L: "Substitution versus production coefficients in the theory of economic growth", Econometrica, April 1959; Salter, W E G: Productivity and Technical Change, University Press, Cambridge, 1966.

23. Nelson, R R: "Aggregate production functions and medium range growth projections", American Economic Review, September 1964.

24. For details and references see Kennedy and Thirlwall's excellent survey, op.cit., and Gregory, R G and James, D W: "Do new factories embody the latest technology", Economic Journal, Vol.83, December 1973.

25. Hicks, J R: The Theory of Wages, Macmillan, London, 1932 (revised 1963).

26. Harrod, R F: Towards a Dynamic Economics, Macmillan, London, 1948.

27. For further details see Hahn, F H and Mathews, R C O: "The theory of economic growth: a survey", Economic Journal, December 1964; Beckmann, M J and Sato, R: "Aggregate production functions and types of technical progress: a statistical analysis", American Economic Review, March 1969; Kennedy and Thirlwall, op.cit.

28. See Massell, B F: "A disaggregated view of technical change", Journal of Political Economy, December 1961.

Appendix I:
The measurement of industrial production at the national level

The Index of Industrial Production (IOIP)

The IOIP is an indicator of changes in the aggregate volume of production in the UK industrial sector (mining and quarrying, manufacturing, construction, gas and electricity). In theory it attempts to measure changes in 'work done' as opposed to goods produced. The value of goods produced (gross output) is an inadequate indicator of production changes since it double-counts production of intermediary goods (eg. car lights by Lucas) in the output of completed goods (eg. cars by Leyland Cars). This can be avoided by the restrictive measure of limiting the scope of the index to completed goods only, or using the preferred measure of value added which excludes for each establishment from the sales value, the value of bought-in goods and services. Changes in inventories and stock appreciation are excluded when calculating value added and inputs and outputs are valued at constant prices. By excluding the cost of bought-in goods and services the measure considers only the 'work done' or value added by the enterprise's labour, land and capital, to these bought-in goods and services. Thus, changes in production due to less subcontracting of activities are reflected in this measure, but not in measures of gross output. The inputs and outputs are valued at constant prices to remove the effects of price changes from the changes in money values to leave only measures of physical, or real, production. Owing to the relatively large data requirements for calculating double—deflated net output, the method is not utilised for the IOIP, being only applied for measuring agricultural production. The IOIP is compiled as the sum of weighted **indicators** of changes in double—deflated net output (see Carter et al for principles [1]). The weights and indicators will be discussed in turn, the formula utilised to represent these weighted changes in production being the fixed base Laspeyres, the base now being changed (and weights updated) only every five years.

The weights for the major industrial sectors, mining and quarrying, manufacturing, construction and gas, electricity and water, are derived from the income based estimates of gross domestic product (net output aggregated for the economy) derived for the **National Income and Expenditure Accounts** (CSO, HMSO, annual). Within these main sectors the results of the **Census of Production** are used to broadly allocate the total sectoral net output to about 130 industries given by the Minimum List Headings of the 1968 Standard Industrial Classification. The basis of this allocation is gross value added derived from the returns of the Census of Production, adjusted for stock appreciation. (Gross value added is similar to net output, see Chapter 1, note [1]). Such data is based on returns by establishments on the value of goods produced and goods and services purchased. Whilst suitable weights are thus available at the industry level, the indicators available generally refer to commodities and a need exists to allocate the weights of an industry between a number of commodities produced. A system of quarterly enquiries provides data on the gross output of the particular commodities and this is used to apportion weights between commodities within industries. In cases where gross output is believed to be unsuitable for this purpose further adjustments are made. The changing of weights only every five years is undesirable since the relative importance of different commodities will change within this period and not be taken into account by the index. It is not surprising that rebasing the index leads to inconsistencies. Estimates by Stirling of the change in the IOIP between 1973 and 1977 using 1970 and 1975 (the new base) as weights were —6.7 and —3.4 per cent respectively. The difference of —3.3 percentage points between the estimates was found to be composed of —3.0 percentage points due to reweighting and —0.3 percentage points due to improved data and so forth [2]. An important source of this quite substantial discrepancy stemmed from 'Petroleum and Natural

Gas Extraction' (North Sea Oil), the weight of which was much greater in 1975 when the industry began producing in substantial quantities. As a major growth industry the rebasing of the index attributed a larger weight to this growth, thus enabling the Sunday Times Business News (25/8/1978) to feature the headline (on the effects on the economy as a whole) "Britain's Growth Rate Boosted by Whitehall Setting New Base Year".

The aforementioned weights are applied to (multiplied by) indicators of changes in production of around 280 commodities (these being in turn built up from about 700 indicators. The first estimate of the (monthly) IOIP is published a month following the end of the period to which it pertains. Provisional indicators are used for this result, the estimate being updated as more reliable information becomes available. About half of the provisional results of the index (by weight) are based on actual data from monthly returns, the remainder being estimated. For the final estimates of the index about 35 per cent of the indicators are derived from an extrapolation of quarterly series; 25 per cent from monthly estimates based on limited samples and, therefore, later bench-marked to quarterly or annual returns and 40 per cent from monthly data (further details of revisions and the basis of extrapolation are given in Perry [3]).

Two main categories of indicators are used for the index, those based on quantities produced and those based on quantities delivered or sold. The latter are affected by changes in stocks of finished goods and adjustments for this are made on a quarterly basis. Whilst the physical quantities of goods produced (eg. number of table jellies) or sold (eg. number of tipped cigarettes) are employed as indicators an alternative formulation used is the deflated value of goods produced (eg. deflated value of aerospace equipment) or sold (eg. deflated value of hand tools and implements). Physical quantity indicators are suitable for well defined goods and do not require price adjustments. Deflated value series cover a wide range (if not the total output) of an industry being deflated by a price index which may not cover all items on the assumption that excluded items experience similar price changes to included items – not as unrealistic an assumption as assuming similar production changes. Some account may be taken of new products and quality changes through this indicator. Input indicators, raw materials and employment, are not employed in the final results of the index, though are used for the provisional results. The use of employment as an indicator merits particular concern, given one application of the index is to relate changes in production to changes in employment to measure labour productivity. Table 1 shows the demise of input indicators and increased preference for deflated values of sales. Figures in brackets are provisional estimates for the 1975 based index; all other figures are final results. Source: Stirling, p.94 and CSO, p.6 [2] and [4].

Table 1, Appendix 1

Types of Indicators used for the IOIP

Percentage of total weight

Type of Indicator	1975 based index	1970 based index	1963 based index
<u>Output indicators</u>			
Production – quantities	24.0 (25.4)	26.7	38.4
– deflated values	24.0 (20.9)	17.0	14.0
Sales or deliveries –			
– quantities	9.2 (6.4)	6.5	4.9
– deflated values	42.8 (40.7)	47.3	29.3
<u>Input indicators</u>			
Materials used	-(3.1)	0.8	11.1
Employment	-(3.4)	1.7	2.3

145.

The use of output indicators assumes that changes in the quantity (or quantity index) of inputs is equal to that of outputs if the (value added) weighted index of changes in these indicators is to equal double-deflated value added. Results of the index are published in the **Monthly Digest of Statistics** (CSO; HMSO) for main industrial sections and 23 separate categories. Both seasonally adjusted and unadjusted results are available. A historical series of the index is given in **Economic Trends,** November 1973 and further details in Carter et al, CSO and Stirling [1], [4] and [2].

NOTES ON APPENDIX I

1. Carter, C F, Reddaway, W B and Stone, R: The Measurement of Production Movements, University Press, Cambridge, 1949.

2. Stirling, D C K: "The rebased estimate of the index of industrial production", Economic Trends, No.307, May 1979.

3. Perry, J: "Revisions to index numbers of production", Economic Trends, No.307, January 1981.

4. Central Statistical Office (UK), The Measurement of Changes in Production, Studies in Official Statistics, No.25, HMSO, London, 1976.

Appendix II:
Value added as an organisational device

Having outlined the features of the concept of value added in Chapter 2 and noted its variants some management applications of the concept can now be considered.

Value added as the basis of financial incentive schemes and productivity measures

Value added financial incentive schemes are generally based on variations in the ratio of value added to labour costs from a normal or target ratio. The normal or target ratio is established from past accounting records and agreed upon by employers and employees. The bonus fund for a future period would be made up of the value added generated above that expected from applying the target or normal ratio to labour costs in the future period. The bonus fund is apportioned between the company and the employers in predetermined proportions. For example, suppose that the normal ratio of value added to labour costs is established as being 1.5 and that labour costs and value added in the following period are £0.9 million and £1.6 million respectively. Then the bonus fund is the difference between the actual value added realised, £1.6 million, and the value added expected from applying the established ratio to labour costs, that is, 1.5 (0.9) = £1.35 million, namely a bonus fund of £0.25 million.

The advantages of such schemes are as follows. They provide an incentive not only to increase output, but also to minimise the costs of bought-in goods and services. They also tend to involve employees in the total operation of the company — though Morley [1] advocates the application of such schemes to small groups in order than the individual will not be isolated from the link between effort and reward. Value added schemes provide an incentive for employees to reorganise the work process to make it more efficient with respect to production and the utilisation of raw materials. They assist in securing freedom in the deployment of labour and the introduction of new methods and machinery. Since a fixed bonus is distributed amongst employees over-manning is not encouraged. The schemes are applicable to indirect workers and may be combined with other financial incentive schemes, such as piece work. The schemes may also improve the quality of the final goods since poor quality products may affect future sales and therefore value added.

It is of interest to relate the above scheme to piece work incentive schemes based on changes in labour productivity. Assuming relative services provided by capital remain constant, changes in the ratio of the number of physical goods produced to man-hours worked provides a meaningful measure of labour productivity. Financial incentives may be linked to changes in this ratio. However, if a scheme is required to cover products for which a major part of the production process for a number of goods is interrelated, or a plant wide scheme is required, a measure of real production is required based on aggregating the individual goods produced. The advantages of double-deflated value added in this context have been noted above. What needs to be stressed is the differences between a system based on the ratio of value added to labour costs and double-deflated value added to manhours worked. The former measures all components of the ratio, gross output, cost of bought-in goods and services and labour cost at current prices for each period whilst the latter deflates each of these components to provide a physical or real measure. Thus the bonus in the former case may be affected not only by changes in the relative physical amounts of goods produced, goods and services bought-in or labour input, but in addition by changes in the relative prices of any of these components.

Thus, for example, if the price of bought-in goods and services increases at a faster rate than that of goods produced, the bonus will suffer from this adverse movement in

the terms-of-trade of the organisation. It may be considered
that a useful feature is that employees suffer (and gain) from
the adverse (or beneficial) movements in the firm's relative
prices. Whatever the case, by choosing appropriate deflators
the technical means is available to include/exclude the
effects of changes in any of the relative prices of goods
produced, services bought-in and labour - details are given
in Silver [2]. Care should be exercised in the use of
productivity schemes based on ratios of monetary variables
(including value added as advocated by Smith [3]) for changes
in these ratios may stem from changes in real and/or price
components which should be separately identified [4].

Value added as an organisational objective

The generation of more value added has been argued to be a
reasonable objective for an organisation, since increasing
the 'cake' of value added will benefit all:

> " . . . the apparent conflict of interest between
> investors, employees and customers is an illusion. All
> of us are customers wanting better value for money. Most
> of us are employees wanting higher wages and better
> conditions. And most of us are investors through pension
> funds, insurance policies and taxation". [5]

Increasing value added may well provide a greater pool of
income to be distributed as labour remuneration and gross
profits (though if the prices of goods purchased by
employees, relative to the prices of the goods produced,
increase at a faster rate the benefits of increasing value
added may be limited or negative). Furthermore, it is true
that the division between employees as receivers of wages and
salaries and owners of the means of production as receivers of
dividends is not absolute. If labour increases its share of
value added at the cost of gross profits there will be a point
at which pension returns or returns from insurance policies
or future investment (and, thus employment) will suffer.
However, the conflict is far from illusionary. Groups of
employees may, and in the United Kingdom have, made
substantial gains in labour remuneration at the cost of gross
profits and these gains may in many instances outweigh any
losses resulting from return on their own investments. Such
action may have been to the detriment of other sectors of the
community, through higher prices and lower returns to
shareholders, yet it is wrong to believe that real gains
cannot be made by some sectors of the workforce. It may be

argued that in some instances this is not desirable, but this
is not to say it is illusionary — it may be only too real.

Wood [6] continues his argument by noting that:

> "Unlike profit, which has emotional connotations, added
> value can be seen by trade unions and their members as a
> worthwhile objective. The enlargement of added value can
> be recognised as a prerequisite of increases in wages and
> salaries. Wealth must be created before it can be shared
> out. The greater the value of the goods and services
> provided by manpower and capital employed in a business,
> the better off will the community be as a whole."

However, the argument that increasing wage rates may eat
into value added, if value added is not increased, will have
the same emotional connotations for it is clearly evident
that this will be at the expense of the profits. The case can
be identified as resting on a consensus ideology which may not
be realistic:

> "The creation and improvement of added value is the
> primary objective of every organisation . . . profit
> alone is not enough. What matters is the amount of added
> value generated by the efforts and ingenuity of the
> employees in using the assets at their disposal." [7]

It is noted that "profit alone is not enough". Enough for
what? — to a shareholder or lender of funds, profit is enough.
Some organisations may be highly dependent on their ability
to finance future projects (for the welfare of the company as
a whole) and a reasonable rate of profit is necessary to
attract equity and loans. One may question whether the
"primary objective of every organisation" should be to
maximise the rewards to every beneficiary of the distribution
of value added, namely, labour, lenders of funds, government,
shareholders. Maximising the real benefits to employees or
net investment could be conceived of as reasonable though
conflicting objectives for organisations. Interest payments
and depreciation can be considered as necessary commitments,
however, it is questionable whether firms should really seek
to maximise their contribution to the government sector. As a
result of the managerial revolution there is evidence that
divident payments may be considered in terms of a satisficing
as opposed to maximising objective.

Thus, the identification of value added as a primary

objective for an organisation may not be because it is composed of the rewards to the factors of production, but because it may allow real net investment and labour remuneration to be maximised, while satisfying shareholders, and enabling depreciation and tax payments to be met. It is, of course, quite possible for shareholders to become dissatisfied with the satisficing behaviour of management and insist on dividend maximisation as an organisational objective subject to the constraint of allocating a sufficient reward to labour. The point is that maximising the cake may lead to larger shares. However, individual groups may seek to encroach on the shares of other groups especially when value added is decreasing (wages being sticky downwards).

Value added as an analytical framework

Value added statements are now a common feature of company reports providing details of its creation — sales minus cost of bought-in goods and services — and its distribution to the aforementioned sources. Burchell, Clubb and Hopwood [8] have commented on the speed with which the framework became accepted, such statements being incorporated in the reports of 14 companies for 1975–1976 and 90 companies for 1979–1980. The justification for any new framework for the provision of information should, to a large extent, lie with its analytical powers, serving the purpose of providing new insights into pertinent features of the company's operation. Through showing changes in the distribution of income to its recipients a valuable purpose is served. The necessity of data on investment, wages and salaries, etc, is appreciated and increases in the **absolute** amount of these items should be monitored. However, as the income generated by the companies to pay these sources varies, we become interested in the **proportion** of income being allocated to these sources. As such a denominator is needed to represent income available for distribution and value added serves this purpose. From the preceding discussion the identification of the real and price components of many of these variables would be of use to aid our understanding of why value added is changing and how different benefits might accrue from relative price changes.

Whilst the statements provide some analytical power their popularity has, as argued in Burchell, Clubb and Hopwood [9], stemmed more from a desire to gloss over profit and show how much the government and employees receive and how little the shareholders. There is much support for this view from the protagonists of these statements. For example, Woolfe [10] in an article directed to accountancy students, attacks the "partisan view" of profit and loss accounts which treat the return to labour as a cost, rather than a share – thus reiterating the consensus framework apparent in Wood's view of the world discussed above. Woolfe argues that government should be isolated as a separate category to which PAYE, corporation tax, overseas tax, grants received, national insurance (employers and employees) should be included. To include PAYE is clearly an absurdity given its collection by the firm is simply an administrative convenience. Denton [11] has argued from a similar stance for the inclusion of rates. Rather than the statement being used to show returns to the factors of production, land, labour and capital, the framework is being mutilated in an attempt to isolate the government sector. The popularity of the statements can be identified from their promotion of a consensus view and as a mechanism for less government, to quote Denton:

"Management and labour will be provided with a realistic view of the total product . . . Both should see that they have been falsely set in conflict . . . The complete value added statement is therefore the first step in bringing sanity back to collective bargaining."

"When individual companies present statements showing all the claims on value added, then we shall have the aggregate picture for all manufacturing and commerce. We shall have the 'black box' of industrial decline, showing which claims (over and above employment-based taxation) have reduced the share of both profit and net wages and salaries. Taxation in one form or another, as is already clear, will have played a large part." [12]

Consider Table 1 which shows the value added statement of a UK retail distributor, as taken from their Annual Report and Accounts. Denton's argument is well illustrated by this statement. Of the value added generated 43.3 per cent is passed on to government, 38.1 per cent to employees, 3 per cent to shareholders and 15.6 per cent reinvested in the business. The government is identified as being a major recipient of the income generated by the enterprise. Yet the government contributes to a wide range of social goods and services, including defence, law and order, social services, health and education. Many of these services are subsidised or free. A pool of income is required to finance the provision of such services and this may stem from consumers,

Table I
VALUE ADDED STATEMENT

	£'000s		per cent
Value added			
Sales including value added tax		1,601,529	
Sundry items including surplus on sale of properties and other investments		406	
		1,601,935	
Less: Cost of materials and services	1,328,336		
Interest payable less receivable	3,207		
		1,331,543	
		£270,392	100.0
Applied as follows:			
Employees			
Wages, salaries and pension scheme costs	125,394		46.4
Less: Deduction for PAYE and employees' social security contributions	22,332		8.3
		103,062	38.1
Central and local government taxes and levies borne by the Group			
Corporation tax	1,370		
Contributions for social security	13,264		
Rates	9,233		
	23,867		8.8
Taxes and levies collected on behalf of government			
Value added tax on sales	70,921		
PAYE and social security contributions deducted from employees	22,332		
	93,253		34.5
		117,120	43.3
Providers of capital			
Dividends to shareholders		8,164	3.0
Reinvested in the business			
Depreciation	14,641		
Retained profit	27,405		
		42,046	15.6
		£270,392	100.0

employees and employers. The extent of the requirements (size of the public sector) and proportion contributed by different groups is a political question decided (albeit inadequately) by electing representatives to Parliament whose policies accord with majority views. Thus government services may not be conceived of as being a 'drain' on individuals, employees and employers, but a source of services. If health, fire, etc. services were not subsidised by the state, payment would be required by either consumers or enterprises for such privately provided goods or services. The relative efficiency of the public and private sectors may be disputed and the diminished consumer sovereignty acknowledged, but PAYE, corporation tax, social security contributions and rates cannot be dismissed as serving no useful function. As with depreciation, retained profits, dividends and bought-in goods and services it serves a specific function.

Table 1 is devised to maximise the role of the government sector. Note that value added tax (VAT) is included in sales (and thus, value added). Now the determination of the incidence of taxation is relatively complex, but VAT can be generally regarded as a comsumer-based tax [13]. The payment of VAT stems from consumers' income not the income of the enterprise. Thus the sales value should exclude VAT and the calculation proceed accordingly. PAYE is aimed at the employee and is but one source of the employee's expenditure. For administrative convenience it is deducted by the enterprise, though can be paid direct to the Inland Revenue. As such PAYE is part of wages and salaries. Rates are the cost of services and should be included with other bought-in goods and services. The enterprise benefits from an educated, healthy workforce, law and order and fire services and should pay for them. Social security contributions are in theory part of labour remuneration and should be included as such. However, in practice part of this sum is directed to services other than social security and this confuses the issue. The fault lies with the government's use of this mechanism as a general tax on employees and employers. It would be proposed that this outlay, if properly utilised should be considered as labour remuneration, though due to the aforementioned factors the employer's contribution will be allocated as a company based tax (though this is not a general recommendation). A brief outline of the revised format is given in Table II which shows quite different patterns of allocation of value added based on sound principles.

If management wish to promote a consensus image and attack taxation, statements following the format given in Table I may be utilised to help accomplish this. However, the limitations of the framework become all too apparent. Take any of the recipients of the income from value added, isolate it, and blame the company's ills on it. For example, the share of dividends or labour costs, too much retained for investment or put aside for depreciation. The point is that all of these areas are necessary to the company's survival. The government provides a range of services to employers and employees, defence, health and social services etc., which would only be a claim on employers and employees under another name if provided separately. If the purpose of value added statements is to isolate areas of excessive costs a much more detailed breakdown can be afforded by cost accountants.

Table II

REVISED VALUE ADDED STATEMENT

	£'000s	Per cent

Value added

		£'000s	Per cent
Sales (excluding VAT)		1,530,608	
Sundry items		406	
		1,531,014	
Less: Cost of materials and services*	1,337,569		
Interest payable less receivable	3,207		
		1,340,776	
		£190,238	100.0

Applied as follows:

Employees

		£'000s	Per cent
Wages and salaries, pension and social security contributions (employee)		125,394	65.9
Government			
Corporation tax	1,370		
Employer's social security contributions	13,264		
		14,634	7.7
Providers of capital		8,164	4.3
Depreciation		14,641	7.7
Retained profit		27,405	14.4
		£190,238	100.0

*including rates

Furthermore, value added statements cannot identify problems relating to marketing, increased competition, adverse changes in exchange rates, production etc. If properly interpreted such statements provide further insights into some facets of a company's operation — not a panacea for industrial decline.

NOTES ON APPENDIX II

[1] M F Morley, "Value added: the fashionable choice for annual reports and incentive schemes", The Accountant's Magazine, June 1979.

[2] M S Silver, "Alternative financial incentive schemes based on value added", Journal of the American

Management Association: Compensation Review, Vol.II, 1979.

[3] G Smith, "Planning for productivity", Long Range Planning, Vol. 13, April 1980.

[4] On such schemes, see also J B Coates, "Productivity: what is it?", Long Range Planning, Vol.13, August 1980.

[5] E G Wood, "Setting objectives in terms of added value", Long Range Planning, Vol.12, August 1979.

[6] ibid.

[7] ibid.

[8] S Burchell, C Clubb and A Hopwood, "A message from Mars – and other reminiscences from the past", Accounting, October 1981.

[9] ibid.

[10] E Woolfe, "Added value, the economic viewpoint:, Libra, December 1979.

[11] N Denton, "Value added: the accountant's key to sane economics", The Accountant, June 1980.

[12] ibid.

[13] See D Jackson, Introduction to economics: theory and data, Macmillan, London, 1982, pp.412-20.

Index

DATE DUE

16 Nov 84			
GAYLORD			PRINTED IN U.S.A.